Faraz Tayyar-Iravanlou
Fatemeh Kalij
Fatemeh Ghahremani

Generalities of Psychology and Clinical Psychiatry

Faraz Tayyar-Iravanlou
Fatemeh Kalij
Fatemeh Ghahremani

Generalities of Psychology and Clinical Psychiatry

Noor Publishing

Imprint

Cover image: www.ingimage.com

Publisher:
Noor Publishing
is a trademark of
Dodo Books Indian Ocean Ltd., member of the OmniScriptum S.R.L Publishing group
str. A.Russo 15, of. 61, Chisinau-2068, Republic of Moldova Europe
Printed at: see last page
ISBN: 978-620-4-72030-2

Generalities of Psychology and Clinical Psychiatry

By

Faraz Tayyar-Iravanlou

Psychiatric Nurse, School of Nursing and Midwifery, Shahid Beheshti University of Medical Sciences, Tehran, Iran

Fatemeh Kalij

Master Student of Psychiatric Nursing, Isfahan University of Medical Science, Iran

Fatemeh Ghahremani

Master student of Psychiatric Nursing, Urmia University of Medical Sciences, Iran

Faraz Tayyar-Iravanlou

Psychiatric Nurse, School of Nursing and Midwifery, Shahid Beheshti University of Medical Sciences, Tehran, Iran

Fatemeh Kalij

Master Student of Psychiatric Nursing, Isfahan University of Medical Science, Iran

Fatemeh Ghahremani

Master Student of Psychiatric Nursing, Urmia University of Medical Sciences, Iran

This Book is dedicated to

My Family's

First word

Some people think that it is only their body that needs food and nourishment, while the soul and mind also need nourishment and it is important. Psychology is the belief that the human body and soul are interrelated and affect each other. So that whenever the soul is hurt, the body also feels bruised and tired and is not ready to move or do anything. The opposite is also true, meaning that a tired and aching body cannot feel good and pleasant spiritually. In any case, the nourishment of the soul and psyche is also essential for life in order for human beings to achieve peace and comfort. One of the most important things in this regard is to remember God and that we should always keep in mind the mighty Creator and Creator of the universe and know that his memory calms our hearts and trusting and relying on him purifies our souls and brightens Gives. God Almighty has endowed each human being with a special talent, taste and creativity, so we should be grateful for such a gift and use them well in the environment of family, work and society in order to nourish our soul and psyche. Human knowledge in all its stages and advances has not yet been able to provide a substitute for the spiritual and psychological issues that are breathed into God by man and are soothing. Although sciences such as psychology and psychiatry have grown greatly, they have no alternative to this important human issue. Teaching and teaching what we know to others can also be a detail of spiritual nourishment. Participating in charities and financial aid and helping such associations will also have a beneficial effect on our morale. If we can be responsible for doing or being responsible for something in our society, even in old age or retirement age, we will create a positive mood and happiness in ourselves. Participating in literary and artistic centers and circles can also flourish our latent tastes and talents and be considered as a kind of spiritual nourishment. For our spiritual nourishment, we should not neglect to do the pleasant and desired things, and on the other hand, socializing with family, relatives and friends entertains us and gives us a happy and fresh spirit. In this work, we try to examine some of the principles of psychology and psychiatry and examine the relationship between these two branches of science that originated from philosophy.

Content

Chapter I

Introduction

Introduction

Psychology, along with other sciences, is greater than all existing scientific systems, and its roots can be traced back to the fourth and fifth centuries BC, with scientists such as Plato and Aristotle, but according to Herman Binghos (19th century), psychology has a long history but a short history. A German-educated philosopher named Radolf Goslenius coined the term "psychology" until the late nineteenth century. Humanitarian psychology emerged in the 1950s and continued to function as a reaction to positivism and scientific research of the mind. The emphasis of this psychology was on the phenomenological theory of human experiences and it sought human understanding and their behavior through qualitative research. The roots of philanthropic thought and philosophy are phenomenological, and many human psychologists have rejected the scientific method altogether, believing that trying to transform human experience into units of measure would empty all its meanings and connections as a living being. Other theorists of this school of thought include Abraham Maslow, the inventor of the human need's series, Carl Rogers, the inventor of customer-oriented therapy, and Fitz Perls, the inventor and exponent of Gestalt therapy. The advent of computer technology also helped to develop the metaphor of mental function in information processing.

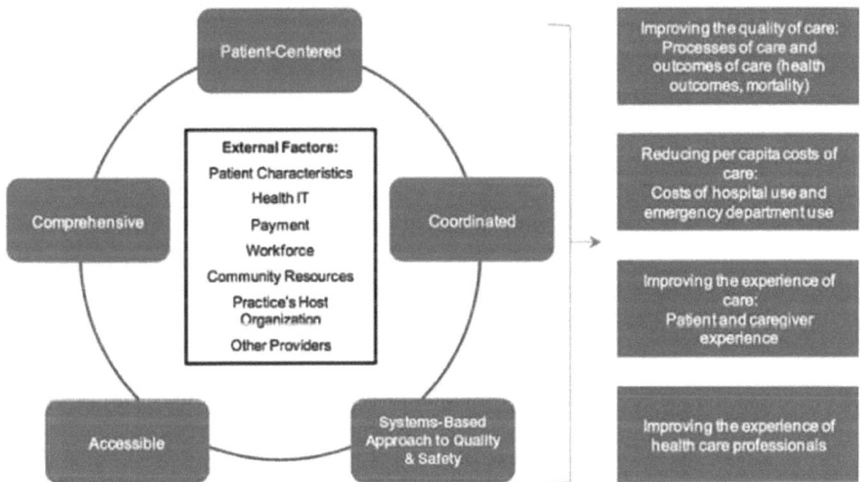

Figure 1. Psychiatry and Psychology

This technology, together with scientific research in the field of mind study and belief in the inner state of the mind, contributed to the emergence of cognitive psychology as a prominent model of the mind. Communication between the brain and nervous system function also became common. Part of the reason for this popularity came from the experiments of people like Charles and Donald Hubb, and part of it went back to scientists' studies of brain injury. With the development of brain function measurement technologies, neuropsychology and neuroscience became active parts of modern psychology. With the involvement of other sciences such as philosophy, computer science and neuroscience to identify and understand the mind umbrella of cognitive sciences as a tool to focus efforts in a constructive way was formed. However, many psychologists were not happy with what was presented as the mechanical models of the human mind and nature. Among those in this circle is Carl Jung, who sought to return psychology to its spiritual roots. Others, such as Sergei and Gerhard Davin, believed that behavior and thought necessarily interacted inherently, and sought to shape psychology into a broader range of social science studies, which are also directly related to the social concept of experience and behavior.

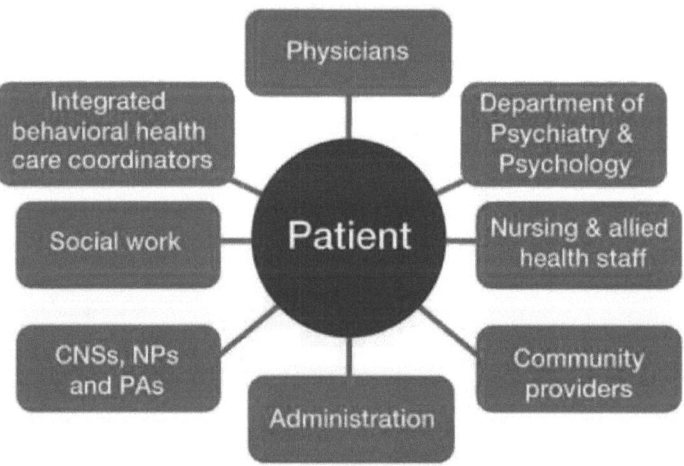

Figure 2. Psychiatry and Psychology, Medical Professionals

The concept of psychology

This word is made up of (Psychology) two parts of psychology (Psy + Chology) which is a Greek word. It is good to know that the word Psyche in Greek means soul (Soul) and does not mean soul, but this word is incorrectly taken in English as Mind and in Persian it follows, we speak English psychology. From a written point of view, psychology should be written separately and with a mediator (half distance) and it is psychologically incorrect to write it.

The nature of psychology

- ✓ Psychology is knowledge.
- ✓ Psychology studies behavior.
- ✓ Psychology examines psychological processes.

Psychology is one of the sciences that seems interesting to the general public and they may pursue it. They may have misconceptions about psychology in their minds, while psychology operates only in the realm of science and faces many limitations. One of these misunderstandings about psychology is equating it with things like divination, mind reading and astrology. However, a psychologist is an ordinary person who, in the field of science he has acquired, can identify some of the incompatible psychological processes and help people to overcome them. In fact, a psychologist does not have the ability to read the mind and predict.

Some people think that psychologists are omniscient and can advise them on the best solution for anything. Psychologists, on the other hand, know how people think, how their problems arise, and how they can lead people to think and feel good. Another misconception about psychology is that a psychologist is going to change your life by talking to you. In fact, a psychologist can help a person for a certain period of time, and this is provided that the person himself is eager to change and accept it. In fact, a psychologist is not a miracle worker. As we have learned from the definition of psychology, psychology is knowledge.

So, like other branches of knowledge, it follows the basics of science (scientific principles). This knowledge examines behavior that is visual (objective) and psychological processes that are imaginary (mental). Behavior is all the reactions that come from living things.

Behavior is obvious and against it are psychological processes, hidden and imaginary (mental). Psychology is a familiar word to the general public. Many of them may think that they know exactly what psychology is and some, on the contrary, are curious to know more about it. In fact, psychology is one of the branches of humanities that tries to know man and help him using scientific methods.

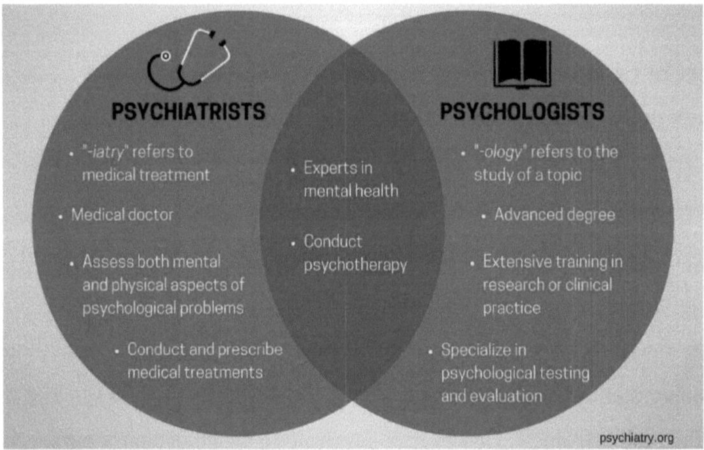

Figure 3. How Does Psychiatry Differ from Psychology?

Psychology is a broad science with a wide variety of areas that include different approaches and theories. A psychologist can help people in many areas, but there is a lot of misunderstanding about this science that prevents society from taking full advantage of the services of this group of professionals.

If we want to define psychology in general, we must say that psychology is a branch of science that studies the behavior and psychological processes of human beings. That is, the subject of the study of everything that is seen in human behavior and every psychological process that exists in his brain. Psychology is a new science with 150 years of life compared to other branches. However, its roots can be traced back to the years BC and ancient Greece.

In fact, psychology is rooted in philosophy and has taken its theoretical foundations to some extent from philosophy. The science of psychology is a vast science. Despite its relatively short history, it includes a wide variety of topics and subfields, and the scope of work of those who enter it varies from research to treatment.

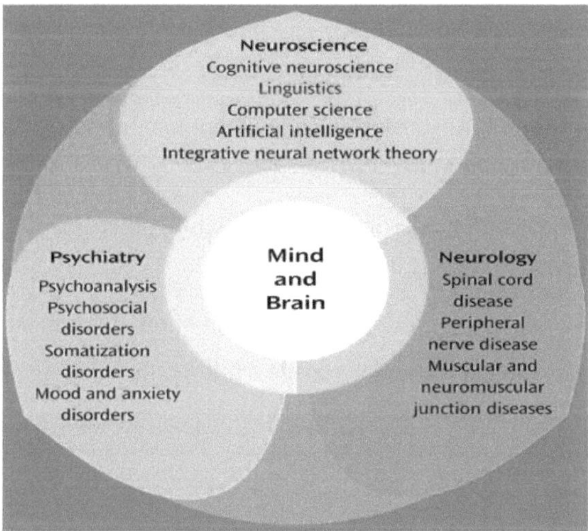

Figure 4. The Integration of Neurology, Psychiatry, and Neuroscience in the 21st Century

Psychological symbols

Psychology is the scientific study of the processes of the mind and behavior. Psychology is a broad field that seeks to understand and explain how thinking, behavior, growth, personality, emotions, motivation, etc. in humans. Gaining a richer and deeper understanding of psychology can help people gain more insight into their actions and a better understanding of others.

There are many different ways to think about human behavior. Psychologists use different perspectives when studying how different people think, feel, and behave. Some researchers focus on one particular school, while others have a hybrid approach that incorporates different perspectives.

There is no complementary view that is better than another. Each simply emphasizes different aspects of human behavior. In the following, looking at the history of psychology, we introduce the most important perspectives that are used today. The symbol (Ψ) is derived from the 23rd letter of the Greek alphabet, just one of the last letters of their alphabet (after psi), which is also the first letter of the Greek word psuche meaning soul or mind. The word is similarly the source of the word psychh. That is where we later got the name of the field of psychology, a science that studies the mind and psychological activities. The symbol of psychology is also the first character of the Greek word psychology mentioned above. This character is the twenty-third letter in the Greek alphabet. Which is called "Sai".

Figure 5. The symbol of psychology

Definition of psychiatry

A psychiatrist is a doctor who specializes in treating mental illness. Because he has a medical degree and is trained in psychiatry, he is one of the few psychiatrists who can prescribe medication to treat mental illness. In addition to psychotherapy, a psychiatrist performs physical examinations and tests, such as a general practitioner.

As part of a mental health team, a psychiatrist can often consult with a general practitioner, social worker, counselor, and psychoanalytic nurses. The psychiatrist also works with the psychologist, but the two should not be confused. The psychologist does not have a medical degree and cannot prescribe medication. In addition, the psychiatrist puts on the agenda the Diagnostic and Statistical Manual of Mental Disorders (DSM 5) developed by the American Institute of Psychiatry, while the psychologist often refers to the DSM 5 on standard psychological tests such as the Multiple Personality Questionnaire.

It relies on the Minnesota Axis and the Rorschach Test. Psychiatry is a branch of medicine that focuses on the diagnosis, treatment, and prevention of mental, emotional, and behavioral disorders. A psychiatrist is a physician who specializes in mental health including substance use disorders. Psychiatrists are qualified to assess the psychological and physical aspects of mental health problems. People seek psychiatric help for many reasons. Problems can be sudden, such as a horrific attack, frightening hallucinations, suicidal thoughts, or hearing noises, or they may be more severe, such as feelings of sadness, hopelessness, or anxiety that never appear or are not a problem in everyday life.

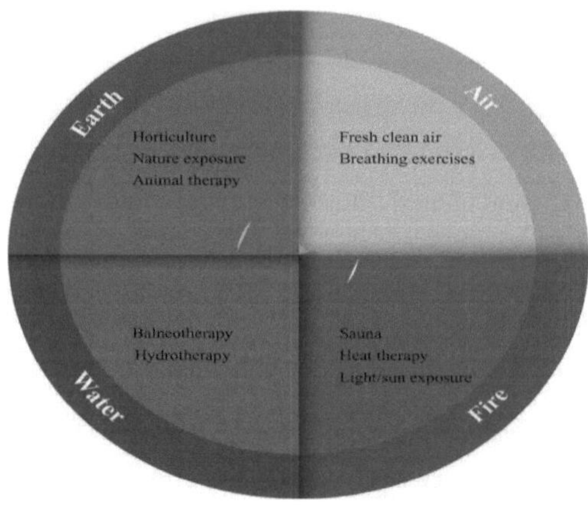

Figure 6. Harnessing the Four Elements for Mental Health

Diagnosis of patients

Because they are physicians, psychiatrists can perform a wide range of medical tests, or psychological and physical and mental tests, along with discussions with patients that help present a picture of a patient. Clinical education provides them with an understanding of the complex relationship between emotional and other medical illnesses and relationships with genetics and family history to evaluate medical and psychological data and to diagnose and work with patients to develop treatment plans. Specific diagnoses are based on the criteria set out in the APA Diagnostic and Statistical Manual. Book Disorders (DSM-5) which includes descriptions, symptoms and other criteria for diagnosing mental disorders.

Psychiatric education

To become a psychiatrist, one must complete a medical university and take a written test for a government license to practice medicine and then four years of internship in psychiatry. The first year of an internship is usually spent in a hospital working with patients with a wide range of medical conditions. The psychiatrist then spends at least another three years learning to diagnose and treat mental health, including various forms of psychotherapy and the use of psychiatric medications and other therapies. Training takes place in hospital, outpatient and emergency rooms. After completing an internship, most psychiatrists take a written and oral examination by a psychiatrist and neurologist to become a psychiatrist. They must be re-approved every 10 years. Some psychiatrists also try special specialized training after four years as a general psychiatrist.

Their training may be in the certificate:

- ✓ Child and adolescent psychiatry.
- ✓ Surgical Psychiatry.
- ✓ Forensic psychiatry.
- ✓ Addiction Psychiatry.
- ✓ Pain medication.
- ✓ Psychological medicine (mind and body).
- ✓ Sleeping pills.

Some psychiatrists choose more training in psychoanalysis or psychological research.

Where do psychiatrists work?

Psychiatrists in various fields including private practice, clinics, public and psychiatric hospitals, university medical centers, social organizations, courts and prisons, nursing homes, industry, government, military settings, rehabilitation programs, rooms There are emergencies, health plans and many other places. About half of psychiatrists in the United States maintain private practice, and many psychiatrists work in a variety of settings. There are about 45,000 psychiatrists in the United States.

What is the difference between a psychiatrist and a psychologist?

When a person encounters a problem (for example, an educational problem with their child), they first ask a friend or older for their opinion, and that friend makes points based on his or her limited experiences that may or may not be helpful. After that, if a person has a better awareness and insight, instead of going to ridiculous acts (such as profanity and astrology), he goes to a professional and, for example, tries to solve his problems by reading a book or article.

For example, he reads a book about educating children, and of course, that book is usually not complete and has not been compiled specifically for us, so in the next step, the person will contact a counselor. Of course, telephone counseling can be a useful solution, but because face-to-face contact There is no face, no good feeling is experienced and usually generalizations are made.

So, the next step is to go to a counselor. The counselor also tries to come up with solutions, and if the problem persists, you should use a psychologist to examine the problems and unique abilities and abilities to choose a simple way in life. Now, after comprehensive psychological examinations and providing appropriate solutions, the person realizes that somewhere in his brain has a problem. You should now go to a psychiatrist to get your hormonal status back by taking certain medications, or ask a neurologist to examine you and perform surgery if necessary, so that you can see your psychologist again.

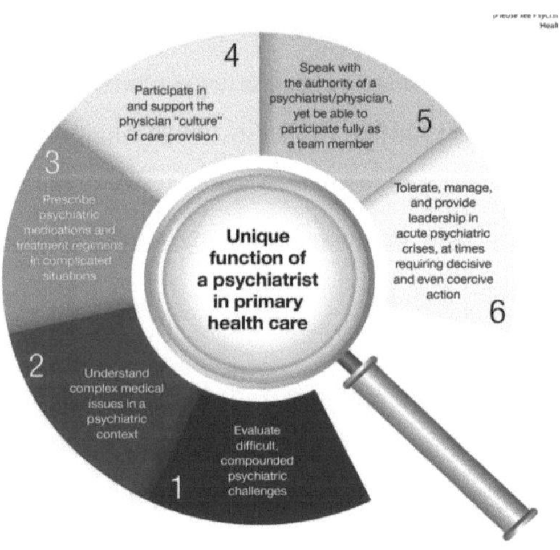

Figure 7. Pin on Adult Autism

A psychologist usually has an advanced degree and is mostly in clinical psychology and often has extensive training in research or clinical practice. Psychologists treat mental disorders with psychotherapy, and some specialize in psychological testing and evaluation. Both psychiatrists and psychologists work in the field of psychiatry, yet they have different functions. The first is a doctor and after graduating from general medicine, he enters the field of psychiatry and finally is called a psychiatrist or neurologist. The latter (psychologist) has studied in a field of humanities.

Psychology has various branches, one of which is related to the treatment of patients and is called clinical psychology. The psychiatrist is responsible for diagnosing the problem or illness and managing the treatment based on the diagnosis. In other words, by considering the various aspects of the individual's problems, he should be able to identify the physical, psychological, family or social origin of the problems and, if there is a disease, distinguish it from similar cases. He or she may send the client to the lab for a diagnostic test or use diagnostic electroencephalography or imaging techniques. After determining the diagnosis, he must select and apply the most appropriate treatment method or methods.

These methods include prescribing medication, performing psychotherapy or counseling, and in some cases using a device or tool for treatment. The psychiatrist may refer the client to a master or clinical psychologist to perform psychological tests or perform psychotherapy, and in some cases seek the help of a social worker or occupational therapist.

In many cases, the desired result will not be achieved without benefiting from such a team. The psychiatrist uses a variety of methods to determine whether a person's symptoms are psychiatric or the result of a physical illness or a combination of the two. Therefore, it is necessary for the psychiatrist to have comprehensive information in the field of general medicine, psychology, neurology, biology, biochemistry and pharmacology. Perhaps a psychiatrist is more skilled than any other physician in communicating between patient and physician and is trained to use psychotherapy and other communication therapy methods to effectively diagnose and control mental illness. Treatment may be outpatient or hospitalized in a psychiatric hospital. The range of types of mental disorders is wide and in general it can be summarized as follows:

- ✓ Anxiety disorders include generalized anxiety disorder (GAD).

- ✓ Practical obsessive-compulsive disorder (OCD).
- ✓ Panic disorder (PD), phobia and social anxiety disorder (SAD).
- ✓ Personality disorders include borderline personality disorder (BPD).
- ✓ Narcissistic personality disorder (NPD).
- ✓ Practical obsessive-compulsive disorder (OCPD).
- ✓ Paranoid Personality Disorder (PPD).
- ✓ Mental disorders include bipolar psychosis, schizophrenia.
- ✓ Emotional schizophrenia and substance use disorder (SIPD).
- ✓ Specific learning disabilities include attention deficit hyperactivity disorder (ADHD) and dyslexia.

Psychiatrist and Psychotherapy

This method is used for both the diagnosis and treatment of mental illness. The psychiatrist meets with the patient on a regular schedule to discuss problems, behaviors, thoughts, emotions, and relationships. The psychiatrist tries to help the patient find solutions to problems by discovering thought, behavioral patterns, past experiences, and other external and internal factors.

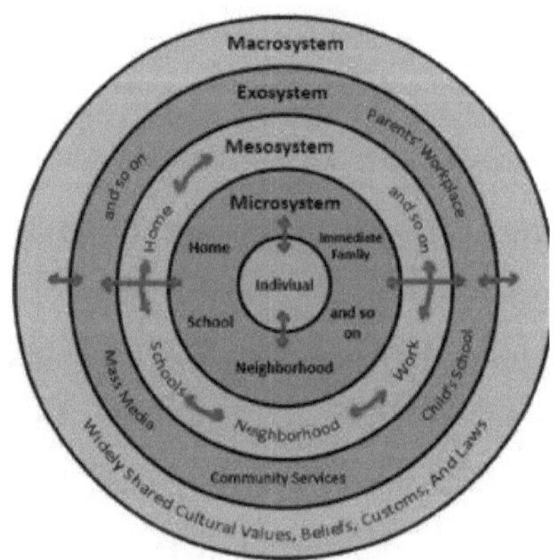

Figure 8. Consultant clinical psychologist

In this method, people can meet with a psychiatrist alone or as part of family or group meetings. Psychotherapy may or may not be given over a period of time, depending on the diagnosis or the severity of the symptoms. According to a 2007 study published in the Journal of Clinical Psychology, at least 50% of people with major depressive disorder will benefit from regular psychotherapy.

Statistics show that 10 to 14 million Iranians have experienced some kind of psychological problem at least once in their lives. "According to WHO statistics, at least one in four people in the family suffers from psychiatric disorders, and family members are usually involved in patients' problems, but in addition to the cultural problems that exist in this field in the country and the patient," said Ali Moin. Refusing to see a psychiatrist another problem facing the field of psychiatric treatment is the length of treatment, which in many cases causes patients to leave treatment. Experts acknowledge that most psychiatric medications are covered by insurance, but non-pharmacological treatments are not covered by insurance.

Unfortunately, these non-pharmacological sessions for treating patients have high costs that are not covered by insurance. On the other hand, it can be noted that psychiatry is a branch of medicine that talks about the diagnosis, treatment and prevention of mental illness. The concept of illness is clear to people, but the concept of psyche may not be very clear.

This may seem strange to people at first, because in our literature the word psyche is always confused with the word soul. In the poems, these two words are next to each other, and dictionaries also use these two words synonymously, but after the emergence of psychiatry, we have to provide a more precise definition. Spirit has one meaning in literature, but the definition of spirit is something else. The Prophet (PBUH) also said about the soul that "I am the command of the Lord". The subject of discussion about the soul is usually in the faculties of philosophy, humanities, and the religious and spiritual fields. Psychological discussion is also within the scope of work of psychiatrists and psychologists. From now on, what we talk about the psyche is the brain activity.

For example, seeing is the result of eye activity and other areas involved in vision. As long as the brain behaves properly, we are also mentally healthy, and if there is a malfunction in the brain, mental illness will occur. Mental illness is a wide range of problems that human beings suffer from, from states such as anxiety, depression, and anxiety, to more severe states, in which the person loses contact with the realities of the environment. Psychiatry is the youngest specialized medical field. Of course, this does not mean that there is no record of it. In the history of Iranian medicine, we have high peaks such as "Abu Ali Sina" and "Razi" who are familiar with mental illnesses and have written articles about it. For example, in the book of Ibn Sina's law or Khwarazmshahi reserve, mental illnesses are mentioned exactly. However, at that time these diseases had other names.

For example, when Boualisina talks about these diseases, he calls them brain diseases. Abu Ali Sina's view of mental illness is very close to what science has reached today. So, note that the history of this science in our country is longer and Europe has just reached these achievements. In fact, we have been a leader in this field in the past. Mental illness covers a wide range.

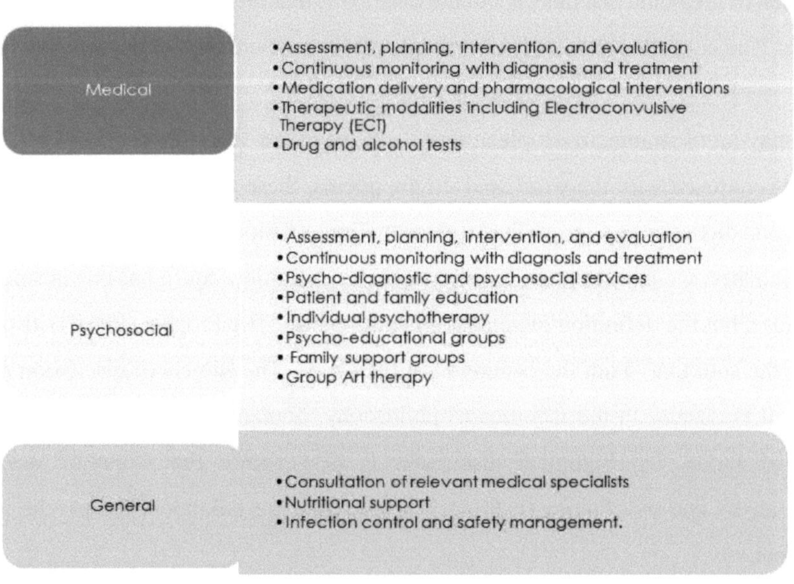

Figure 9. Inpatient Care

The characteristics of these diseases are among the human information today. Statistics on the number of people with mental illness and the number of people in need of treatment in this area vary from country to country, but in general it can be said that about a quarter of the population in each country needs psychiatric services each year. This means that one in four people needs psychiatric services.

Our people think that someone who has a psychiatric problem and needs to see a psychiatrist means that his or her normal life is disrupted, and perhaps that is why many people are reluctant to see a psychiatrist even if they need help. The reason for this perception in people is that in the West, the youngest branch of medicine is psychiatry. That is, not many years have passed since the beginning of teaching psychiatry as one of the specialties in Western medical schools, unlike medicine itself, which has a very long history both in Iran and in the Western world. The first Iranian-educated psychiatrists in the West, like the survivors of Dr. Hossein Rezaei, Dr. Abdolhossein Mirsapasi, and Dr. Chehrazi, returned to Iran from Paris in 1996. In the first decade of the present century, the Iranian government sent students abroad to study various new disciplines, including psychiatry, where they became neurologists, and the late Dr. Rezaei returned to Iran before anyone else.

Even when they returned, the statistics on the number of mentally ill people worldwide were not very accurate. For example, the late Professor Bash of Sweden took the first statistics of the mentally ill in Iran, which was about four to fifty percent. The reason is that at that time, people were considered mentally ill who were completely mentally disturbed and were displaced on the streets or ran away from home and were not accepted by the community and harmed people.

These people form a group of mentally ill people called psychopaths. This means that those people have fundamental problems in judgment, behavior, emotions, perceptions and thoughts, and as a result, their contact with the realities of life is cut off. About 45 years ago, other researches on the epidemiology of the mentally ill were conducted in Iran. The most important of these was research conducted by the late Professor Haraton Davidian and his colleagues in the city of Rudsar in northern Iran, and it was the first time that the rate of mental illness was higher than the previous figure. This is because the new classifications consider all psychiatric disorders to be mental illness. For example, those who had anxiety, sporadic physical pain, stress, and insomnia without a physical injury also became mentally ill.

What are Psychological Labels?

People should be recognized and told that, contrary to what is being said, mental illness is not the equivalent of an insult. Mental illness is the equivalent of heart disease. Mental problems are also problems such as heart, lung and digestive problems. We must make sure that people do not use the word psychological as an insult and humiliation. Psychology has very different definitions. One of the more appropriate definitions for psychology is the science of studying and recognizing human behaviors, both normal and abnormal.

Figure 10. Translating research findings into clinical practice: a systematic and critical review

The first time this definition was introduced in Iran in the new era was at the Faculty of Literature, where the late Dr. Ali Akbar Siyasi was a professor of psychology. Initially, psychology was called epistemology, and Dr. Siyasi used the word "psychology" as the equivalent of the French word "psychology." Psychology is the science that studies human behavior. Students also usually study psychology in the faculties of literature and humanities or psychology.

Undergraduate or graduate students in psychology are actually introduced to the basics of general psychology, and in this course, they study a wide variety of subjects, such as educational, social, clinical, educational, and so on. Clinical psychology is close to psychiatry because after obtaining a bachelor's degree in clinical psychology or another bachelor's degree, they spend a master's degree in clinical psychology and in psychiatric hospitals. The practical units of this orientation are in the patient's bedside, i.e., they have not gone to medical school, but after receiving their doctorate or master's degree, they become part of the psychiatric treatment team in the psychiatric hospital. The only field of psychology in which graduates have the right to participate in the treatment of the mentally ill in accordance with Iranian law and international standards is clinical psychology.

Of course, the work of other psychologists is very valuable in its own right, but they are not allowed to treat patients. Unfortunately, for some reason, for some reason, a group of people who have not learned clinical psychology according to customary education have been visiting patients in the city, and this is one of the harms to people's mental health.

The main tasks of a psychiatrist

- ✓ Assess the mental and physical condition of patients to determine the nature and extent of behavioral, emotional and mental disorders.
- ✓ Evaluate the medical and psychiatric history of patients in order to better diagnose the disease and prescribe the best treatment.
- ✓ Perform various tests to diagnose the disease and find the best treatment.

- ✓ Prescribing medicine and holding the necessary treatment sessions until the patient recovers.
- ✓ Collaborate with other specialists, including physicians, psychologists, and… to comprehensively treat the patient until he or she reaches full recovery.

Psychology and other sciences

Sometimes the work of neurologists overlaps with the work of psychologists, and because people avoid the word psychiatry, it is called neurological disorder, or it is called neurological disorder. This word and this concept are more acceptable to people, but it should be known that a neurologist is someone who has passed his specialized course in the field of neurology and has read theoretical courses related to this subject and the scientific branch.

The work of these people is very difficult and valuable, but some people turn to these people for treatment of their mental illness. According to the rules, any doctor in Iran can treat any disease until he makes a mistake, but a person with mild and severe psychiatric disorders, at the request of himself or his family and due to ignorance and avoidance of mental stigma, A neurologist (neurologist) comes in who may be wasting some time on this path. Because the main work of neurologists is other diseases that exist in the neurological series.

Another mistake people make is going to a neurosurgeon. Suppose a person has a headache and the headache is caused by a brain gland and is operated on and the headache is treated. After treatment, this person tells the whole family that the headache has improved with brain surgery, and others who have headaches and may be due to other disorders go to a neurologist. Another thing that makes mental patients waste their time is that mental illnesses can appear with complaints in different parts of the body. Such as complaints in the cardiovascular system, respiratory diseases, gastrointestinal and….

This patient may have this problem for years and see a doctor frequently. Sometimes a blood test can detect the type of disease, such as anemia. In many cases, those who go to the specialist with pain, the doctor tells them that they are healthy. Saying no one has heart disease encourages a mentally ill person who complains of heart pain to go to another doctor.

The golden age of healing is important in the treatment of all diseases. The golden time is the first period of the onset of the disease, when the disease is not yet chronic, and if there is sufficient knowledge from doctors and people in that period and treatment is started on time, the treatment will have a good result.

Figure 11. Ketchmed-training

Another important issue in the treatment of mental illness is psychotherapy and treatment with pills, which is very important to know. So, what about psychotherapy? Which class is responsible for this? Classically, psychotherapy began with Sigmund Freud, a neuroscientist himself who developed many theories that had been around for years, but now new theories have been proposed and applied.

After Freud started doing this and psychotherapy was introduced as a new treatment, there were still no drugs for it. Currently, 1% of mental illness treatment is medication and 2% is non-pharmacological, and psychotherapy uses various methods, but the most tangible and well-known method among people is psychoanalysis. Psychiatrists and psychologists who are clinically trained and have passed the relevant units in their course can also work in psychotherapy.

It is better for the treatment team to be in charge of the treatment team with a clinical psychologist working with the team, but the situation should not be such that those who have not passed the relevant courses and are not clinical psychologists intervene in the treatment work. Because according to Iranian law, those who have a license from the Ministry of Health can enter this field.

Psychotherapy Fellowship

For psychiatrists who want to engage in psychotherapy, a psychotherapy fellowship course was launched at Roozbeh Hospital affiliated to Tehran University of Medical Sciences. Psychotherapy work is usually done sporadically by psychiatrists, but psychiatrists who wish to acquire more skills can take this course. Now, after years of review and revision, the Ministry of Health and Medical Education has allowed the fellowship course for general psychiatrists to be launched as a specialist, and this will be helpful. Because it makes the treatments performed are comprehensive.

According to the existing laws, psychotherapy is a medical matter and according to the law and custom, those who have received the relevant education in the medical universities of the country and are licensed by the Ministry of Health and Medical Education can do so.

Areas of work of psychology

All human behaviors and psychological processes arise from his mind. Therefore, the main task of psychologists is to study the following:

- ✓ Study of human behavior and its consequences.
- ✓ Study of psychological processes such as feelings, emotions and thoughts.
- ✓ A study of the brain and its functions and its role in behavior and psychological processes.
- ✓ Addressing mental disorders and adjustment problems.
- ✓ Mental Health and Mental Health Assessment.

- ✓ Help improve human performance.
- ✓ Crisis management and intervention.

Branches of Psychology

Clinical Psychology: Clinical psychology is a branch of psychology that evaluates and treats mental illness, abnormal behavior, and psychological disorders. Clinical psychology combines knowledge, theory, and practice to identify, prevent, and treat adaptation problems, disabilities, and promotes adaptation, correction, and personal growth. A clinical psychologist focuses on the intellectual, emotional, biological, psychological, social, and behavioral dimensions of human performance throughout a person's life, based on different cultures and economic and social levels. Clinical psychology can also help us understand, prevent, and treat psychological disorders caused by anxiety or dysfunction, and improve our personal well-being and development. Clinical psychologists often work in private clinics, but they may also work in community centers and universities. Other clinical psychologists work in hospitals or mental health clinics as part of a collaborative team that may include physicians, psychiatrists, and other professionals.

Cognitive psychology: Cognitive psychology examines internal mental processes such as problem solving, memory, learning, and language, and this branch of psychology assesses how thinking, perceiving, interacting, remembering, and learning. Cognitive psychologists also look at how information is processed and stored. Practical applications of this branch of psychology include how to improve memory, increase decision accuracy, or how to set up training programs to enhance learning. Cognitive psychologists often use an information processing model to describe how the mind works and show that the brain stores and processes information like a computer.

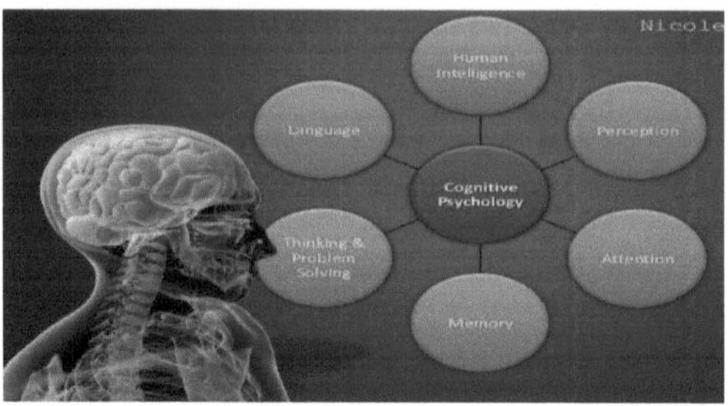

Figure 12. What is Cognitive Psychology?

Developmental psychology: This branch of psychology is the scientific study of the regular psychological developments that a person experiences throughout life as growth, and this branch of psychology focuses not only on infants and young children but also on adolescents, adults, and the elderly. Some of the elements of this branch are: motor skills, problem solving, moral comprehension, language acquisition, emotions, personality, self-concept and identity formation. Psychology, on the other hand, examines the development of intrinsic mental structures versus learning through experience, as well as how a person's personality traits interact with environmental factors and how they affect human development. Developmental psychology also overlaps with topics such as linguistics.

Criminal psychology: Criminal psychology is a specialized field that deals with topics related to psychology and law, and those who work in this field of psychology apply psychological principles to legal subjects, which may include the study of criminal behavior and attitudes or direct work in Be a court system. Criminal psychologists perform a variety of tasks, including testifying in court, evaluating children in suspected cases of child abuse, preparing children for testimony, and assessing the mental competence of criminal suspects. In many cases, people working in criminal psychology are not necessarily criminal psychologists. These individuals may be clinical psychologists, school psychologists, neurologists, or counselors who use their psychological expertise to provide testimony, analysis, or advice in legal or criminal cases.

Health psychology: Health psychology specializes in how biological, psychological, and behavioral factors affect health and disease, and the field of health psychology focuses on health promotion as well as disease prevention and treatment. Health psychologists are interested in promoting health in various fields. Not only do health psychologists promote healthy behaviors, but they also work in the field of disease prevention and treatment, and they often deal with health-related topics such as weight control, smoking cessation, stress management, and healthy eating. They may also research how people cope with illness and help patients find new and more effective coping strategies.

Organizational industrial psychology: Industrial Industrial Psychology is a branch of psychology that uses psychological principles to research job topics such as productivity and behavior at work. This branch of psychology works to improve productivity and efficiency in the workplace while at the same time maximizing employee well-being and increasing employee job satisfaction. Some organizational industrial psychologists work in areas such as human factors, ergonomics, and human-computer interaction. Psychologists working in the field of human factors focus on improving how people interact with products and machines inside and outside the workplace. They may help design products that minimize damage or create workplaces that increase accuracy and safety.

Personality psychology: Personality psychology is a branch that studies the patterns of thinking, feelings, and behaviors that are unique to each individual. Classical theories of personality include Freud's theory of personality psychoanalysis and Erickson's theory of psychosocial development. Personality psychologists may study how various factors, including genetics, parenting principles, and social experiences, affect how personality develops and changes. Researchers in the field of personality psychology are interested in understanding many of the forces influencing how personality develops and manifests. They are also interested in learning more about changing personalities throughout their lives. Areas of personality psychology include constructing a coherent picture of the individual and his or her major psychological processes, examining individual psychological differences, and examining human nature and psychological similarities between individuals.

Social psychology: Social psychology seeks to explain and understand social behaviors and addresses a variety of topics including group behavior, social interactions, leadership, nonverbal communication, and social influences in decision making. This psychological orientation focuses on topics such as group behavior, social perception, nonverbal behavior and body language, adaptation, aggression, and prejudice. Social influences on behavior are important topics in social psychology, but social psychologists also focus on how people perceive and interact with others. This branch of psychology is interested in knowing how people's behaviors and feelings are influenced by other people.

School psychology: School psychology is a branch of psychology that involves working in schools to help children deal with academic, emotional, and social issues. School psychologists also work with teachers, students and parents to help create a healthy learning environment and reduce children's fears about school. Most school psychologists work in primary and secondary schools, but some also work in private clinics, hospitals, government offices and universities. Some also offer private counseling, most of whom have a doctorate in school psychology.

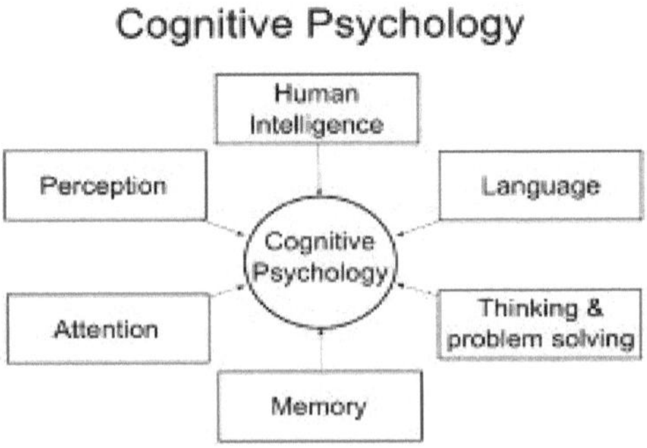

Figure 13. Cognitive Psychology Theory

Online Psychology: Today, people face many problems due to the development of societies and most of the time they get tired of work and life, but they do not have enough time to get counseling and their mood changes day by day and they go through the process of depression. Usually, people become more aggressive and do not enjoy the activities that used to make them happy, and they look for a way to get rid of this problem. That's why online consulting is on the rise. Research has shown that people with depression respond better to online counseling and are treated. Many people are afraid or embarrassed to talk about their problems in front of someone else and for a thousand other reasons refuse to do so.

Neuropsychology

Neuropsychology deals with the structure and function of the brain in relation to psychological behaviors and processes, and if a disease involves lesions in the brain, a neuropsychologist or neuropsychologist evaluates and records the electrical activity of the brain. Neuropsychological assessment is used to determine if a person is experiencing behavioral problems following a suspected or detected brain injury. These results could enable a physician to offer a treatment that may help the individual make possible advances in the pathology that has occurred.

The purpose of psychology

Every knowledge has goals and objectives that the scientist strives to achieve. The basic goals of psychology are:

1- Description

The first goal of psychology is to simply describe behaviors and psychological processes. By describing psychological behaviors and processes, we can better say whether the behavior is normal or abnormal. Psychologists use a variety of methods to describe. Examples include natural observation methods, case studies, correlations, contexts, and therapist reports. Psychologists' express views and theories based on descriptive sentences and concepts that are based on hypotheses. So, with the help of description, we understand the "what" of behavior and psychological processes. With the help of description, we get answers to some questions.

2- Explanation

Psychologists seek explanation after description. We use description to understand what psychological behavior and processes are, but to explain "why" we need an explanation. With the help of description, we can get to know about suicide, aggression and what they are, but we need an explanation to find out why they occur.

3- Prediction

The third goal of psychology is to predict behavior and psychological processes. We want to predict how people will behave or think in different contexts. For example, some people believe that aggression or watching aggressive behavior reduces the feeling of aggression, but psychological research has shown the opposite view. Based on these studies, it can be predicted that a child who tends to watch violence at the age of 9 behaves more aggressively at the age of 18 than other peers.

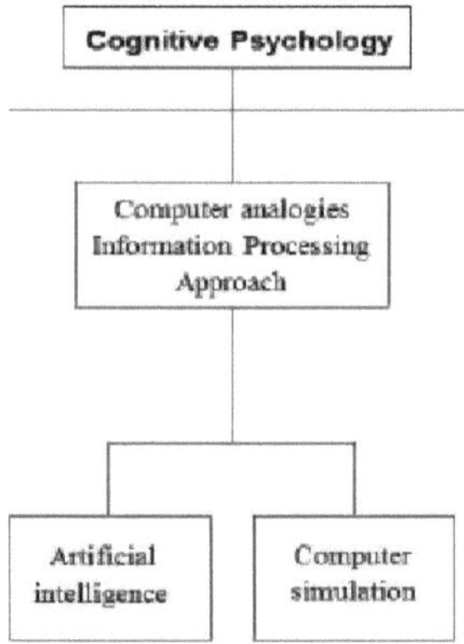

Figure 14. Cognitive Psychology Model by McLeod (2015)

4- Control

The highest goal is the psychology of control. With control, we can prevent or reinforce abnormal behaviors. So, we can say that psychologists are looking for answers to the following questions:

- ✓ What is a behavior? (Description)
- ✓ Why does this behavior occur? (Explanation)
- ✓ When does this behavior occur or will it occur? (Forecast)
- ✓ What effect does this behavior have on a person's life and how can we prevent negative effects on life? (Control)

Psychological approaches

Psychologists use different points of view to study and understand humans. In fact, each of them, according to different philosophical bases, follow different schools and approaches in psychology. Each approach has a specific point of view on some issues, explains them and suggests a specific form of treatment in dealing with mental disorders. The predominant approaches to psychology include the following:

1- Psychoanalysis

Psychoanalysis is one of the first known "approaches" to psychology, founded by Freud. Psychoanalysts initially deal with people's past through certain processes and believe that by deeply examining the past and unconsciously examining people, they can solve a person's problems. This approach has undergone many changes over time and new approaches have emerged from it.

2- Behaviorism approach

It is one of the first known approaches that focuses on the observable behavior of the individual. For a behaviorist, it does not matter what goes on in the mind, just what is seen, measured, examined, and ultimately plans to change. With behavioral therapy, they discover specific rules of behavior and use specific behaviors to change it.

3- Cognitive approach

In cognitive approaches, behavior and psychological issues are examined through how individuals are identified. The focus of this approach is on the flow of people and their maladaptive thinking is examined and changed in treatment.

4- Biological approach

The biological approach, as its name implies, is the study of biological processes that lead to behavioral and psychological changes, and in fact the study of the brain is a priority in this approach.

Origin and history of psychology

The origins of modern psychology can be traced back to the fourth and fifth centuries BC in Greece. Philosophers such as Socrates and Plato have asked various questions about human psychological life. There have also been traces of this knowledge in Iran, China, India and Egypt.

What is clear is that approaches such as cognitive, behavioral, and biological in psychology have originated from the ideas of philosophers such as Plato, Socrates, Hippocrates, and others. It is not surprising, then, that the knowledge of psychology is inextricably linked with the knowledge of the mother, which is philosophy. Most (but not all) psychologists believe that the birth of Danesh psychology (scientific psychology) took place in 1879. That was the year that Wilhelm Wundt set up the first psychological laboratory in Leipzig, Germany. Wilhelm Wundt is called the father of laboratory psychology. The history of psychology as a science of studying human behavior and mind goes back to ancient Greece.

There is also evidence of the study of this knowledge by the ancient Egyptians. The science of psychology was considered part of philosophy until 1879, when it was studied as an independent science in Germany and the United States. Psychology borders on the sciences of philosophy, sociology, neuroscience, physiology, and the humanities in general.

In 1879, Wundt established the first laboratory for psychological research in Leipzig, Germany. In 1881 Wundt published the first journal to introduce the results of psychological research. In 1890, William James published Principles of Psychology. In 1892, Stanley Hall founded the American Psychological Association. In 1904, Ivan Powell demonstrated how conditioned responses could be created and, by introducing classical conditioning, paved the way for the emergence of response stimulus psychology. In 1905, Alfred Binet developed the first intelligence test in France. In 1909, Stanley Hall invited Freud to speak at Clark University in the United States, and as a result, Freud's growing fame was officially recognized, especially in the United States. In 1913 John B. Watson wrote the Classical Behaviorism Statement, in which he stated that psychology should only study the observable behavior of living things. The use of intelligence tests became widespread between 1914 and 1918, during the years of World War I.

In the 1920s, Gestalt psychology reached its peak of influence among psychologists as well as the science of psychology. Scientific psychology emerged in the last quarter of the nineteenth century, but psychological exploration began at the same time as the rise of philosophy. Psychological thinking has been a part of philosophy for more than 24 centuries, from the time of ancient Greek philosophy to the end of the nineteenth century. The term psychology, like many psychological information, has Greek roots and consists of the two words "psyche" meaning soul or mind and "logos" meaning cognition or study, which literally means psychology, the study of the soul, and cognition or the science of the soul. The invention of this term is attributed to Philip Melancton in the years 1497-1560.

Other names were used simultaneously for this science in the eighteenth and nineteenth centuries, some of which are: philosophy of mind, self-knowledge, and psychology. Throughout its long history, philosophy has sought to understand human nature and human mental life. All the ideas and solutions that philosophers have offered to explain human nature, mind, consciousness, processes and mental activities such as feeling, perception, learning, cognition, reasoning, will and emotion form the structure of philosophical psychological thought. Because this thinking developed by philosophical rather than empirical methods, it is called pre-scientific psychology. Physiology also played a major role in building the new psychology.

The influence of physiology mainly led to the separation of psychology from philosophy and its emergence as an independent science. In fact, the history of psychological thought and historical perspectives on the nature of the psyche and behavior goes back to one of the works of the ancient Greek philosophers, Aristotle, which was written under the title "The Subject of the Psyche". Other ancient Greek thinkers also contributed to the development of this science. Democracy, for example, declared about 400 BC that we could base our behavior on body and mind.

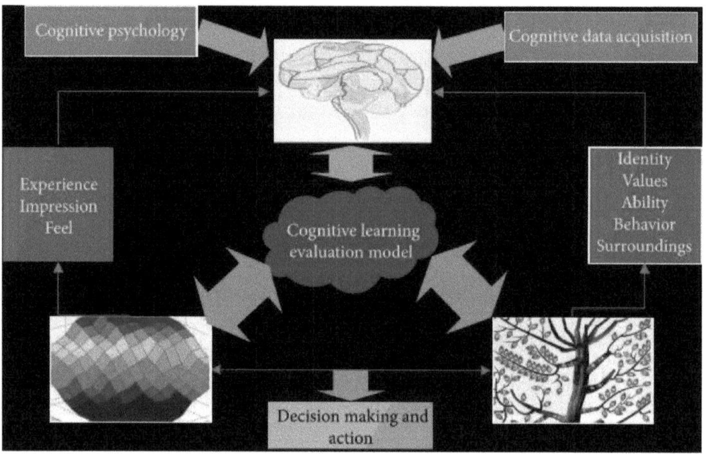

Figure 15. Relationship between Cognitive Learning Psychological Classification and Neural Network Design

Figure II

The growth of psychology in the world

Psychology in Germany

Experimental psychology began in Germany in 1879, when Wilhelm Wundt opened the first official psychology laboratory in Leipzig. Wundt's permanent and exclusive reputation in the history of psychology is not because of his system of thought or theories, but rather because of the mediation of scientific psychology.

From philosophy and physiology, he created this new science called "physiological psychology". Wundt focused more on the "awareness" experiment. Wundt's role as an experimental psychologist is undeniable, and in fact he can be considered the founder of the new psychology. History of the heyday of German empirical psychology without considering men. As interest in the psychology of cultural sciences increased in the 1920s, interest in laboratory psychology declined, and so did the impact and scientific support for psychology in German universities.

In 1927 a group of German psychologists demanded that universities pay more attention to psychology, but after 1933, the tendency to ignore and condemn nineteenth-century psychology increased. In 1933, Karl Stummief, the last pioneer of German psychology, died. German scientific psychology was left without a strong leadership. As a result, with the rise of the Nazi regime, it could no longer play a role in advancing psychology.

Psychology in America

The theory of evolution quickly found its way to America in the late nineteenth century, and American psychology was more influenced by and guided by Darwin and Galton than Wundt. Wundt had trained all early American psychologists in his own style of psychology. However, on the way back to these young Americans and across the Atlantic at the end of the century, very little was transferred from Wundt's true psychological system.

When these new psychologists returned to the United States, they established a type of psychology that bore little resemblance to what Wundt had taught them. American culture was oriented toward pragmatism and utilitarianism, and people valued something that had a practical benefit. The country expected psychology to be applied, and it achieved this through the efforts of James, Hall, Cattell, and other pioneers of American psychology. They studied how the mind works, not what it is made of. They took psychology to the real world of education, industry, advertising, child development, and clinics, and made it functional. The work of American psychologists was influenced by three factors:

- ✓ Wont Laboratory Experiments.
- ✓ Darwin's evolutionary hypothesis.

The concept of the natural Gaussian probability curve, all three of which are reflected in laboratory experiments, developmental (genetic) studies, and the statistical method of American psychology. The founders of psychology in the United States, with the exception of a few, were willing to pursue their experiments independently. Stanley Hall, for example, 1844-1926, and James McKinney Cattell (1860-1944) both studied with Levent in Leipzig. Hall promoted the Child Study Movement in the United States, and in 1892 was elected the first president of the American Psychological Association. In contrast, his colleague Cattell had a significant influence on the movement of psychological tests and the study of the psychology of individual differences in the United States. Psychology grew in the United States with the country. The dynamic and vibrant evolution of American psychology from 1880 to 1900 is an evolving event in science.

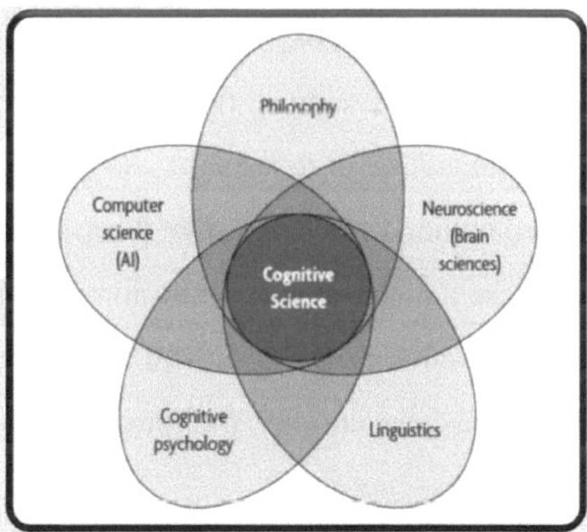

Figure 16. Cognitive Processes Chapter 8. Studying Cognition Language Use Visual Cognition Problem Solving

Psychology in England

There was little effect of Wundt's laboratory psychology in the United Kingdom. In 1869, under the influence of Darwin's theory of evolution, Francis Galton undertook a series of pioneering studies of individual differences, including historical research on the evolutionary method. He also studied the concept of test to measure a specific trait and developed the correlation method as a statistical method for analyzing figures and numbers. Following Galton, Carl Pearson pioneered statistical methods in 1857-1936 and Vaspirman pioneered statistical methods in 1945-1863, with England taking the lead.

Psychology in France

French psychologists have been interested in studying abnormal behavior from the beginning. In 1792, Paynel freed the mentally ill from shackles in a Paris hospital, and in 1801 he wrote a treatise on mental alienation, treating mental illnesses as treatable as physical illnesses. Charcot, Burnheim, Ribo, and Jeanne were among the leading psychologists to hold high positions in the history of French psychopathology and psychiatry. French scientists also showed great interest in the study of hypnosis (artificial sleep), which was first called animal magnetism by Mesmer in 1779.

Reasons for the emergence of the field of psychology

In today's industrial world, there is almost no activity or profession that is not dependent on human understanding and thought, so psychology has created an inseparable link with modern human life. In addition, the growth of science, technology and the level of public welfare has led to more time for thinking and thinking. Thus, problems, problems, and even emerging diseases arise among human thoughts and mindsets that redouble the need for solutions, treatment, and prevention, the solution of which is pioneered today by psychology.

The existence of different branches of psychology is itself a convincing reason for claiming that on the one hand human behaviors are different and on the other hand this behavior is manifested in different ways at different ages and times and to recognize human behavior at different ages and times. And in different cases we need to be aware of their psyche. For example, it is very likely that most of us will have children. If we learn the psychology of growth, we will know what the different stages of life are like. We will know about sperm formation, embryonic development, events during childbirth, infancy, possible retardation and ways to prevent them, and this awareness will help us raise children and thus a healthier generation and ultimately have a healthier society.

In other words, awareness of the mental states of human beings in each stage of childhood, adolescence, youth, adulthood and old age, will cause a response commensurate with the expectations of each member of society. All parents claim that they are raising their children well, while some set certain hours for the child to eat and sleep, study and play, and others set the child free. Some parents threaten to cut off love and rejection of the child, and it is even seen that they corporally punish their children. There are parents who leave their children free to do whatever they want. These parents believe that children should be released to prevent them from becoming entangled. In contrast, there are parents who never give such permission. Which group is doing the right thing is a question that can be answered in the field of educational psychology?

General perceptions of psychologists and psychiatrists

Some people think that psychologists and psychiatrists are the same or are not well aware of the differences between them. A psychologist is generally a person who starts studying psychology from the moment he enters the university and learns the specialized field of psychology. Such a person in graduate school more limited his field of work and focuses more specifically on a particular part of psychology, but a psychiatrist is a person who after 7 years of study in medicine and after obtaining his medical degree to continue his education and specialization, Chooses psychiatry and studies in the field of mental disorders for about 4 years. Psychiatrists generally approach psychological issues from a biological point of view, and their main job is medication for mental disorders. Most psychiatrists deal with severe mental disorders that require medication and inpatient services in psychiatric centers, but psychologists do not prescribe medication and examine issues from a psychological, social, and cultural perspective.

In fact, it is the main specialty of psychologists who learn its skills well during their school years. Some people think going to a psychologist means going crazy. But who is crazy? People use the word crazy to refer to a person whose behavior is abnormal or who is struggling with certain problems. The fact is that in psychology we have no concept called insanity and we do not actually study it. Psychology is the study of behavior and mental and psychological processes. Therefore, its circle is wider than it is limited to a certain stratum. Everyone has a special benefit of mental health. There are psychological problems such as depression, anxiety, difficulty adjusting in some situations, problems in human relationships such as marriage and parenting and many other issues in all human beings. So, a psychologist can help anyone to improve their life and improve their mental health.

Figure 17. What is Psychology Q & A

On the other hand, people with more severe problems can use the services of psychologists to overcome their problems. In fact, seeing a psychologist does not necessarily mean having severe problems, and even if this is the case, it is very natural for a person with severe problems to seek solutions. Like a person who has cancer and goes to the doctor to get rid of the problem, and at the same time a person who has a cold or a broken arm goes to the doctor.

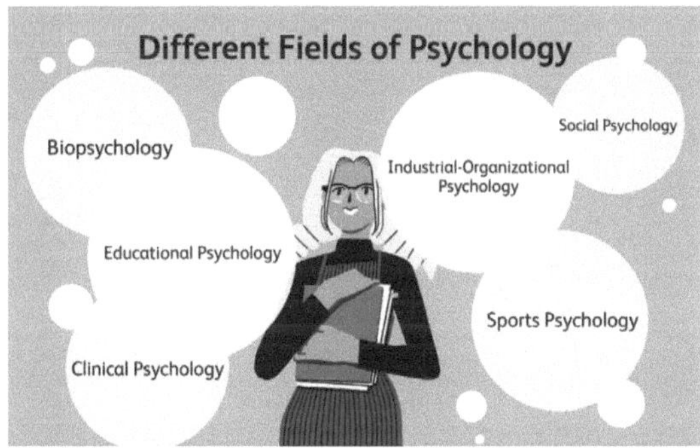

Figure 18. The Major Branches of Psychology

Chapter III

General applications of psychology

Ethics and the development of ethics

Ethics is a set of common values and beliefs of society about the rules and principles of behavior. Adolescents, like children, often exhibit behavioral patterns in the family and educational environment, as well as imitating the behavior of some of their admired peers and adults. Moral growth is not merely a function of temporal and chronological age, but is the product of the cognitive development of thought. Kleberg (a psychologist in the field of ethics) stated that the way people argue about an issue does not reflect the content of the individual's response to a problem's moral maturity and moral development. When given the choice between obeying the law and defending the rights of individuals, those who are highly morally advanced defend individual rights. The stages of moral development from the point of view of Kelberg (the famous psychologist) include six stages, which are expressed in three general levels:

1- Stages of moral development

A) Pre-customary level: At the pre-customary level, moral principles are externally controlled. For example, children accept the rules of those in power, such as parents and teachers, and evaluate the actions of individuals by their consequences, and the behaviors that are punished are bad and the behaviors that are rewarded are good.

B) Orientation of punishment and information: At this stage, children can hardly consider two points of view on a moral issue. As a result, they ignore the intentions of individuals and focus on fearing those in power, such as parents and teachers, and avoiding punishment as reasons for behaving morally.

C) Instrumental goal orientation: Children become aware that people can have different views on a moral issue, but at first this children's awareness of moral issues is very objective. They consider personal action to be in their personal interest. For example, you do this for me and I will do it for you.

D) Customary level: People at the customary level still consider obedience to social rules important, but not for personal gain and for their own benefit. Children believe that maintaining the existing social system and maintaining order in society will ensure positive relationships in society.

E) "Good boy, good girl" orientation: The "good boy, good girl" orientation stage is also called the ethical principles of interpersonal cooperation. At this stage, people want to maintain the love and approval of friends and relatives by being a good person, that is, trustworthy, loyal, polite, helpful and lovable.

F) Orientation to maintain social order: At this stage, the person has a larger perspective, such as maintaining social rules. At this stage, children think that social norms and laws should be applied equally to everyone, and that every member of society has a duty to obey the laws. People at this stage believe that the rules should never be broken.

G) Post-customary or moral level: post-customary or moral level goes beyond the unequivocal support of the rules and regulations of their society. They define moral principles in terms of abstract principles and values that apply to all situations and societies.

H) Orientation of the social contract: In the orientation phase of the social contract, individuals consider laws and regulations as means of flexibility to achieve human goals. Individuals at this stage can visualize other options for their social order and emphasize fair methods for changing the law. At this stage, people understand that the rules can be changed for the greater welfare of the people of the society.

Figure 19. Psychology-Related Careers to Consider

I) Orientation of universal moral principles: In this stage, the action of the hands of individuals is defined by conscience, that is, in this stage, conscience grows, which is valuable for all individuals, regardless of the law and social agreement for all members of society. Conscience is an abstract value. People who develop a conscience believe that the value and dignity of each individual should be respected.

Recognize body language

1- Tongue

Body language refers to the non-verbal signals we use to communicate. According to experts, these non-verbal cues make up a large part of our daily communication. From facial expressions to body movements, things we do not say can still convey information to the other person. It has been suggested that Buddy Langweig may account for between 60 and 65 percent of all communications.

Although reading and interpreting body language is important, it is also important to pay attention to the context and environment. In many cases you have to focus on a set of signals instead of focusing on a single action. You will learn more about how to recognize body language, but before that you need to know more about this concept. Body language, also known as nonverbal communication, is a complex body signal system for interacting with our emotions, thoughts, and mental states. This is because the system is so complex that it encompasses various channels such as the face, limbs, body posture when sitting or standing, and even how far we are from others. Each of these channels can transmit different messages.

They send signals to others about specific or general emotions, as well as specific cognitive processes and physiological states. When we put all these channels and their signals together, we realize the complexity of nonverbal and windy language behavior. Reading other people's body language is very exciting because it brings different messages to us. When we talk about communication, we often mean what we say. However, interpersonal communication goes far beyond the clear meaning of the words and information they convey through the message.

Communication includes both intentional and unintentional implicit messages that are conveyed through nonverbal behaviors. Non-verbal communication can convey more information and meaning beyond what we say.

In fact, some estimates suggest that about 70 to 80 percent of all communications are nonverbal. In defining body language, this concept refers to the use of bodily behaviors, states, and methods of nonverbal communication that are often instinctive rather than conscious, whether consciously or not, constantly interacting with nonverbal cues. Send and receive. All your nonverbal behaviors, sitting posture, your voice, your eye contact rate send important messages to the other person. These signals can make others feel comfortable and make the other person trust you or attract them to you, or they can have the opposite effect and confuse or upset the other person. These messages do not stop when you pause.

Even when you are silent, you still have non-verbal communication. In some cases, what comes out of your mouth and what you show through your body language are two completely different things. If you say something that your body shows otherwise, the listener may feel that you are not being honest. For example, when you say yes, but do not shake your head. When confronted with these conflicts, the listener must decide whether to trust your verbal behavior or your nonverbal behavior. Because body language is a natural, unconscious language that reflects your true feelings and intentions, the listener is more likely to choose your nonverbal message after reviewing it.

2- Eyes

The eyes are referred to as the windows of the soul. Because the eyes have a great capacity to convey people's thoughts and feelings. When you are talking to another person, paying attention to their eye movements is a natural and important part of the communication process. Some common body language issues that you may notice are whether the person in front of you has direct eye contact or avoids staring at you. How much does he blink or are his pupils dilated? Observe the following eye signals when evaluating body language:

A) Staring: When a person looks directly into your eyes during a conversation, it shows his interest and attention. Prolonged eye contact, however, can be threatening. On the other hand, cutting off eye contact or often looking elsewhere may indicate that the person is distracted, uncomfortable, or trying to hide their true feelings.

B) Blinking: Blinking is normal, but you should also pay attention to this point in recognizing body language, whether the person blinks a lot or a little? People usually blink faster when they are upset or upset. Low blinking may indicate that the person is deliberately trying to control their eye movements. A poker player, for example, may blink less to show how excited he is about his cards.

C) Pupil size: Pupil size can be a subtle non-verbal communication signal in recognizing body language. While the amount of light in the environment controls the pupil dilation, sometimes emotions can also cause minor changes in pupil size. For example, have you heard of seductive eyes? The term is used when a person is attracted to another person. In this case, the pupil of the eye is very wide.

D) Face mode: Think for a moment about how many messages a person is able to convey with a face mode. A smile can indicate approval or happiness. Frowning can be a sign of unhappiness or dissatisfaction. In some cases, our facial expressions may reflect our true feelings about a particular situation. While you are saying that you are fine, your face may say something else to those around you. Some examples of emotions that can be expressed through the face are: happiness, sadness, anger, surprise, hatred, fear, confusion, excitement, desire and humiliation.

A person's facial expressions even help us to see if we trust what he or she is saying. One study found that the most reliable face is a slight increase in eyebrows and a slight smile. Face shape is also one of the most universal forms of body language. The facial expressions used to express emotions are similar all over the world. Research even suggests that we judge the intelligence of others based on facial expressions. A study of body language has shown that people with slimmer faces and more prominent noses are more likely to be perceived as smarter. Also, people with happier faces and smiles were found to be smarter than those with angry faces.

3- Mouth

Oral postures are also essential in reading a person's body language. For example, chewing on the lower lip may indicate that the person is experiencing feelings of anxiety, fear, or insecurity. If the person is yawning or coughing, covering the mouth may be an attempt to be polite, but it may also indicate an attempt to cover up opposition. Smiling may be one of the most important signals of body language, but smiles can also be interpreted in different ways. A smile may be real or it may be used to express false happiness, sarcasm or even pessimism.

Observe the following signs when interpreting body language orally:

A) Shrinking lips: Closing the lips tightly can be a sign of reluctance, opposition or mistrust.

B) Lip biting: People sometimes bite their lips when they are worried, anxious or stressed.

C) Covering the mouth: When people want to hide an emotional reaction, they may cover their mouth to prevent a smile or grin.

D) Up or down the mouth: A slight change in the mouth can also be a subtle indicator of a person's feelings. When the mouth is slightly upwards it can mean that the person is feeling happy or optimistic. A downward-facing mouth, on the other hand, can be a sign of sadness, grief, opposition, or even an obvious crooked mouth.

4- Arms and legs

Arms and legs can also be helpful in recognizing nonverbal communication. Closing the arms can indicate a person's defense. Also, when you step on your feet, it may indicate that you do not like the other person or feel upset with him. Excessive opening of the arms can also be an attempt to look bigger, while keeping the arms close together is an attempt to shrink and isolate. Note the following signals:

- ✓ Holding hands may indicate a person's defenses, self-protection, or self-closure.
- ✓ Standing with your hands on your hips can be a sign of readiness and a sense of control. This signal also means aggression.

- ✓ Tying your hands behind your back may indicate that you are feeling bored, stressed, and even angry.
- ✓ Taping fingers can be a sign of boredom, impatience or frustration.
- ✓ Taking a step can indicate that you want to shut yourself down or need to protect your privacy.

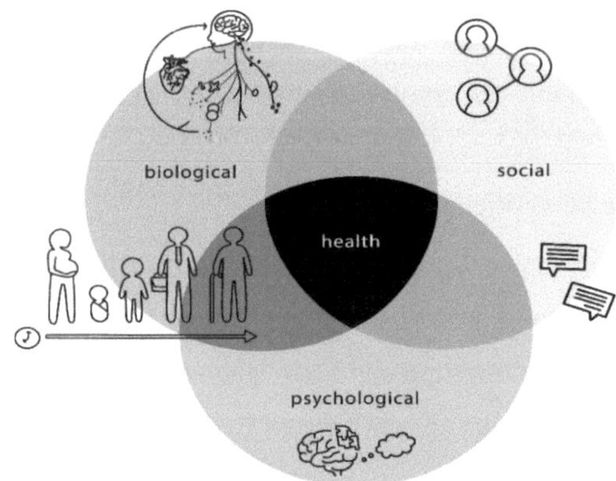

Figure 20. What is Health Psychology?

Why is body language important?

Nonverbal communication and how you listen, look, move and react show the other person how much you care about them and how successful you are at listening well. When your nonverbal cues match what you are saying, trust and agreement in the relationship increase, but when this is not the case, it causes tension, mistrust and confusion. If you want to have a better relationship, it is important not only to pay attention to the body language and non-verbal cues of others, but also to be sensitive to your own body language. Regarding the importance of body language, it is important to know that body language plays five roles, which are:

A) Repetition: Body language repeats, thereby reinforcing the message you convey verbally.

B) Contradiction: body language can be inconsistent with the message you are trying to convey. So, it shows the listener that you may not be telling the truth.

C) Substitution: Body language can replace a message. For example, your facial expressions usually send a clearer message to the other person than the words you say.
D) Complete: Buddy Langweig may add or complement your verbal message. For example, as a boss, if you gently pat your employee on the shoulder while admiring him, your message will be more effective.
E) Highlighting: Body language may highlight or emphasize a verbal message. For example, tapping on a table can convey the importance of your message.

Can body language be artificial?

There are many books that will give you advice on how to use body language. For example, they may tell you how to sit, close your fingers, or shake your hand to look confident. In answer to the question can body language be artificial? We have to say that the truth is that such tricks are unlikely to work unless you are really confident. You cannot control all the signals you send. However, this does not mean that you have no control over your nonverbal cues.

For example, if you disagree with what the person is saying, you can use negative body language to disprove what they are saying. Like touching your chest, avoiding eye contact or tapping your foot. You can consciously try not to send negative signals to communicate effectively and avoid defending the other person. For example, be open-minded and try to listen well to what the person is saying.

General body shape (Posture)

Overall body shape can give you a lot of information about how a person feels as well as tips on personal characteristics when reading Body Language. Including whether the person is confident or receptive and obedient? For example, sitting straight shows that a person is focused and attentive to what is happening. Sitting with the body bent on the other hand shows that the person is bored and indifferent.

Open mode

The open position includes an open and comfortable upper body, which indicates friendliness and receptivity, willingness and self-confidence.

Closed mode

Closed position involves hiding the upper torso by squatting or crossing the arms or legs, and can indicate hostility, unfriendliness, and anxiety.

Personal space

Have you ever heard of someone pointing out that they need personal space? Have you ever felt uncomfortable with someone close to you? The term application is coined by anthropologist Edward T. Edward T. Hall refers to the distance between people in interaction. Just like facial and body movements, personal space between people conveys important information to us. It should be noted that the level of personal distance can vary from culture to culture:

A) Intimate distance of 15 to 45 cm: This distance often indicates a closer relationship between people and their sense of comfort with each other. For example, this gap exists in romantic relationships. It usually happens in that intimate contact such as hugging, talking on the phone or touching.

B) Personal distance 45 to 121 cm: This physical distance usually occurs between family members or close friends. The closer people are to each other in this personal distance, the closer they are to each other.

C) Social distance 1.21 to 3.65 meters: This level of distance usually occurs with familiar people. This may be less the case with people you know well, such as co-workers you see several times a week, but someone you do not know well with, such as a postman who may meet only once a month. You see, this distance can be closer to 3 meters.

D) Public distance 3.65 to 7.62 meters: This distance is usually present in public speeches. Talking in a class full of students or presenting a project at work are good examples of such situations.

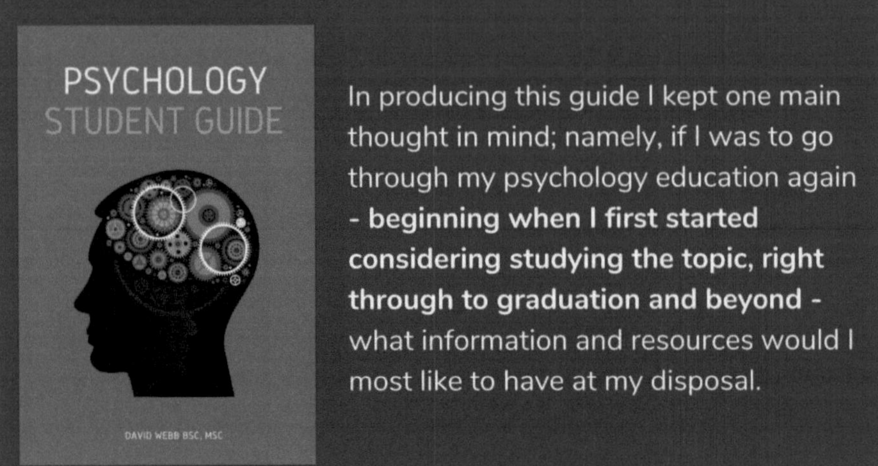

Figure 21. Psychology Student Guide

Psychology and boosting self-confidence

Self-confidence is a term that manifests itself in many areas. From improving mental health to helping people achieve career goals and more. The term is more than a word and is a concept that is associated with mental health, well-being and a positive way of life in the world, and includes both feeling and doing. This concept is a process that includes how one thinks about oneself and others, as well as how one performs in the face of challenges and uncertainties.

Self-confidence is used both in the inner and personal world of a person and in the outer world around him and is related to almost all elements of a happy and satisfied life. People with high self-esteem are those who are aware of their capacity to do something and then do it.

These people do not need the approval of others, and the most important thing for them is to know what they have the capacity and potential to do, and to take advantage of the opportunities that stand in their way. Self-confidence is the attitude you have about your skills and abilities. It means believing in yourself and feeling in control of your life. Be aware of your strengths and weaknesses and feel positive about yourself. You set realistic expectations and goals, you communicate boldly, and you can face criticism. Therefore, this skill is one of the indicators of life skills and means the courage to know oneself, believe in oneself and act according to these beliefs.

Confidence means

- ✓ You evaluate yourself regardless of the mistakes and things you have done or are not doing.
- ✓ You feel good about yourself.
- ✓ Value yourself regardless of your flaws.
- ✓ You are brave enough to be brave.
- ✓ You know that you deserve the respect and friendship of others.
- ✓ You know and accept yourself and your strengths and weaknesses.
- ✓ What does not show confidence?

What does self-confidence not include?

- ✓ Believing that you are perfect or that you think you should be perfect.
- ✓ You expose yourself to unrealistic expectations and standards.
- ✓ Having a life without pain and problems.
- ✓ Being selfish.

Is self-confidence the same as self-esteem?

Self-confidence and self-esteem are very similar terms, but they are not the same. Self-confidence can be defined as positive feelings about oneself and the world that affect one's performance. Self-esteem is sometimes defined as the degree to which a person values himself or herself. There is also another concept called self-efficacy, which means a person's belief in the ability to do a task. These three concepts are not the same, but they are related. Self-esteem emphasizes one's feelings about oneself. Self-efficacy emphasizes the degree to which one believes one can do something. Defining self-confidence means emphasizing self-acceptance and how one behaves in the world because of that acceptance, and is probably a combination of self-esteem and self-efficacy.

Why do we need confidence?

Obviously, this skill has many benefits for people, especially in their career path. Some people and job positions need people who have high self-esteem. For example, jobs such as advocacy and judging, journalism, management, public relations, acting, teaching, marketing management, sales staff, etc.

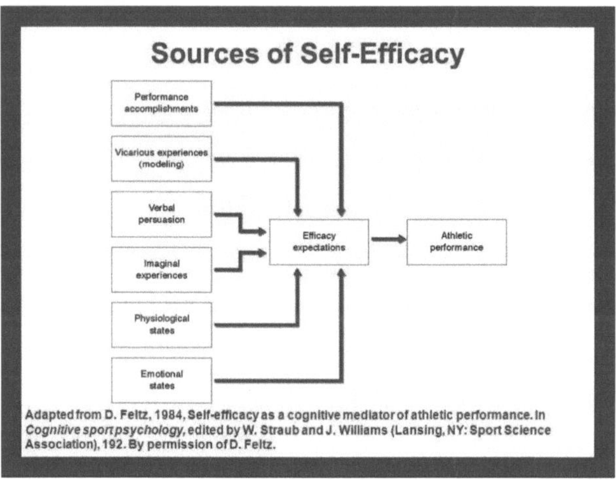

Figure 22. Sports psychology: self-confidence in sport

In fact, it is a skill that everyone needs. People with high self-esteem can express themselves freely and create a lasting image of themselves with the employer in job interviews. Because of the direct relationship between self-confidence and competence, people trust those who have high self-esteem. For this reason, basic projects and valuable contracts often reach these people. Confidence is a motivating factor that encourages entrepreneurs and pioneers to start new projects. If you have high self-esteem, you can make independent but excellent decisions in your organization or field of work and not constantly worry about your supervisor's orders.

How confident did he look?

Your confidence level is shown in many ways. For example, through body language, how you speak, what you say and so on. A person with high self-esteem believes that what he is doing is right, even if others criticize him for this behavior. He likes to take risks and strives for better things. This person accepts his mistakes and learns from them, as well as accepting praise and admiration from others. His body language and body shape also show that he is confident. In contrast, a person with low self-esteem behaves according to what others approve of and does not take risks for fear of failure. He tries hard to cover up his mistakes and hopes to solve the problem before anyone knows about it. In addition to not seeing his inner values, he also refuses to be admired by others.

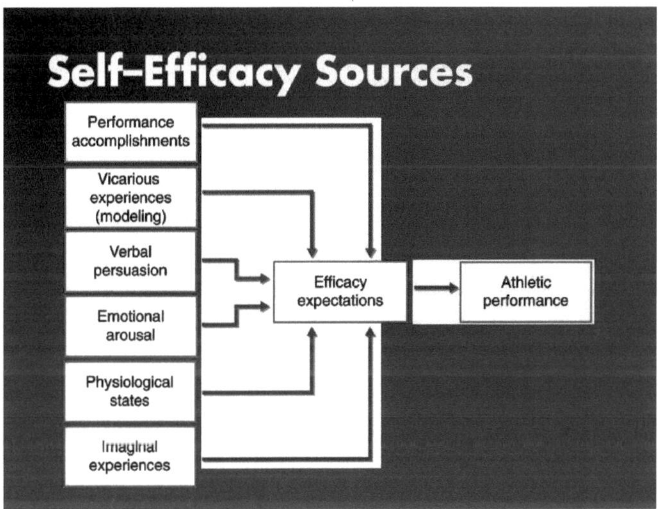

Figure 23. Defining Self–Confidence Self-confidence: Self-efficacy

The relationship between self-confidence and self-esteem

We all know that self-esteem, sometimes called self-esteem and self-worth, plays a very important role in success. Too low self-esteem can make people feel defeated or depressed. It can also lead to unfavorable choices, destructive relationships or feelings of helplessness, but this does not mean that self-esteem is too desirable. Excessive self-esteem in people with narcissistic personality disorder It can be seen. These people feel superior to others and as a result their relationships with others are damaged. The level of self-esteem should not be at the bottom of the top or bottom of the spectrum, but should be in balance. Ideally, you should have a realistic but at the same time positive view of yourself. This feature helps people to have a growing life and achieve self-fulfillment. Various studies have reported the effect of self-esteem on people's general health and its relationship with success, happiness and having positive relationships with others. Self-esteem refers to a person's overall sense of self-worth and, in a way, measures how much one values, approves, and loves oneself. In a simple definition, self-esteem means one's attitude towards oneself and this attitude can be desirable or undesirable. Various factors affecting self-esteem include:

A) Genetics: For example, oxytocin receptors are of two types: adenine and guanine. Research has shown that people who have at least one adenine are more sensitive to stress and have poorer social skills.

B) Personality: Studies have shown that among the five major factors of personality, extraversion, agreement and openness to experience are directly related to self-esteem.

C) Life experiences: For example, a person who has experienced many failures in life or has been abused as a child has less self-esteem than others.

D) Age: Researchers have reported that self-esteem can increase up to the age of 60-70, but after this age it declines. There is also an increase in self-esteem between the ages of 4 and 11 and a decrease in self-esteem in early adolescence.

E) Health: A person with a chronic physical or mental illness usually reports lower feelings of self-worth and self-esteem than other people.

F) Thoughts: Negative thoughts, such as the thought that I am worthless or that I cannot do something right, cause people to fail in relationships and opportunities, which results in nothing but low self-esteem.

G) Social conditions: Because the higher the social status of a person in society, the more respect he receives from others. In this way, his self-esteem also increases with increasing social level.

H) Reactions of others: Being praised and encouraged increases self-esteem. On the other hand, the more a person is criticized and humiliated by others, the less his sense of self-worth decreases.

I) Comparing yourself to others: When a person compares himself to others, he can never win, because there is always a better person. For this reason, comparing yourself to others has no effect other than lowering your self-esteem.

What is an important point in answering the question of self-esteem? That is, it is not a fixed concept, but a flexible and measurable one. This means that we can measure and improve it. Self-esteem can take many forms of your beliefs about yourself. Including evaluating your appearance, beliefs, emotions and behaviors. The level of self-esteem should be balanced and if it is too much, it means that it is unhealthy. This is a problem that exists in narcissistic personality disorder and indicates that the person has extremely low self-esteem, but wants to compensate with a sense of superiority and arrogance.

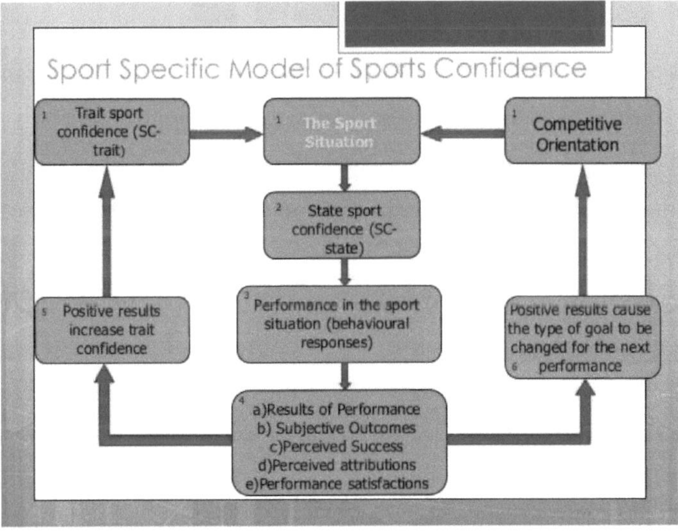

Figure 24. Self-confidence and self-efficacy 2013

The importance of self-esteem

Self-esteem can play an important role in your motivation and success throughout life. Low self-esteem can keep you from succeeding at school or at work because you do not believe you can succeed. On the other hand, having a healthy self-esteem can help you achieve success, because then you have a positive and courageous attitude in life and you believe that you have the ability to achieve your goals.

Regarding the importance of self-esteem, it should be noted that people with low self-esteem will have a painful life, because they feel very worthless and cannot make decisions in the long run that will help them. These people miss life opportunities and have trouble making friends with others and do not even bother to try new relationships. These people also seek the approval of others and show a special image of themselves in cyberspace, which at the same time is highly addictive and deprives the person of the opportunity to make real contact with humans.

Similarly, low self-esteem makes one vulnerable to falling short of the demands of others, and this shows the importance of self-esteem. The two concepts are very similar, but not the same. For example, you may be able to easily appear in front of a crowd and give a speech that shows your confidence, but at the same time you may not feel good about your speech, which indicates low self-esteem. Self-confidence is about whether or not you believe in doing your job, and self-esteem means how much you value yourself.

In fact, if you feel better about yourself because of what you have done, it is a sign of self-confidence, and also if you look at the task ahead of you and believe in yourself to do it, it is still a sign of self-confidence. On the other hand, when you accept the truth of your intrinsic value as a human being, you have self-esteem.

Another important point about the difference between self-confidence and self-esteem is that self-confidence can be easily undermined by a mistake or a negative dialogue. Self-esteem can also be destroyed, but since it has nothing to do with achievement and doing things well, you can rediscover and rebuild it.

Spectrum of self-esteem

Your self-esteem fluctuates according to circumstances and over time. It is natural that sometimes you are disappointed in yourself and sometimes you feel good about yourself. However, in general, the range of self-esteem is such that it shows how you feel about yourself in general, and this feature also increases slightly with age. Consider the following and determine if self-esteem is low or healthy?

A) Low self-esteem: Do not value your thoughts and beliefs and focus on weaknesses and shortcomings and also do not consider your skills and abilities valid. So, you believe others are more capable or more successful. You may have trouble accepting positive feedback, and you may also be afraid of failure and therefore not trying to succeed. You are also afraid of being alone and worried that others will leave you.

B) Healthy self-esteem: When you have healthy self-esteem, it means that you have a balanced and accurate view of yourself. For example, while you have a good idea of your abilities, you know your flaws. When your self-esteem is healthy and based on reality, it is impossible to have too much of it. Pride and a sense of superiority over others indicate insecurity and low self-esteem. As you may have noticed by now, self-esteem is a feeling of self-worth and self-love as a human being and has a profound effect on people's general health. If you feel that you are facing weaknesses in this area, the good news is that you can improve your self-esteem with solutions.

Confidence and social power

Have you ever wanted to reach your goal so that you could not sleep? Most people want to achieve their goals, but they underestimate the importance of self-confidence. This concept means believing in one's own strengths and abilities and is a quality or state of certainty. If you are unsure about your abilities and characteristics, it will be very difficult to convince others to believe in you. Having self-confidence means accepting your flaws and experiencing positive feelings about yourself. A person with this skill acts boldly because he believes in his inherent value. This skill means that although you do not like things in yourself, you love your wholeness. This concept is a deep sense of self-awareness within you that without modern clothes or armor, makes you confident.

Therefore, having self-confidence helps people to be successful and happy in all aspects of life. Although self-confidence can mean different things to different people, it actually means self-belief, and this skill is the result of how we are nurtured and educated. We learn from others how we think and act about ourselves, and this affects how we believe in ourselves and others. This skill also stems from our experiences and how we learn to react to different situations. Self-confidence is not a static concept and can decrease or decrease according to tasks and situations. Because of this we may have more confidence some days.

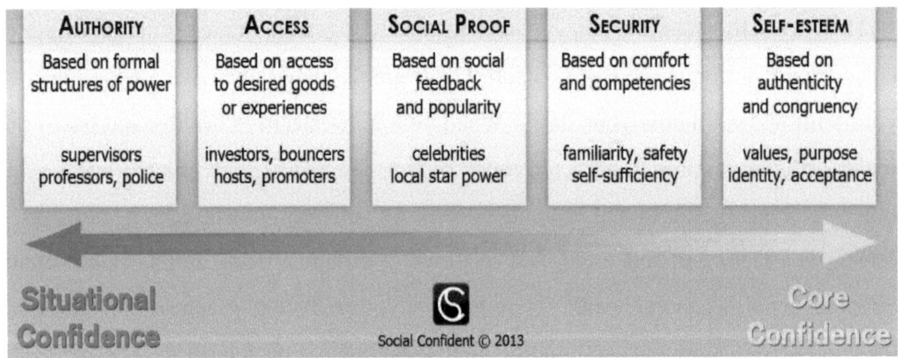

Figure 25. Core confidence vs situation confidence

The relationship between psychology and social resilience

Resiliency is equivalent to the English word Resiliency. In the dictionary, this word means elasticity, reversibility and elasticity. Resilience is derived from physics and means jumping backwards. In fact, resilient people can jump back. They have the ability to survive and even overcome adversity.

In other words, resilience is the capacity to resist stress and crisis. Psychologists have always tried to increase this human ability to adapt and overcome dangers and difficulties. Resilience does not mean that you can live a life without stress and pain. In fact, resilience means the ability to cope with difficult situations and respond flexibly to the pressures of daily life. Resilience does not limit stress or eliminate life's problems, but empowers people to deal with life's problems in a healthy way and to overcome difficulties.

Is resilience teachable?

Resilience refers to a person's capacity and ability to deal with the stresses and hardships of life, but this inner ability of a person to interact with the environment is strengthened and shows itself as a positive characteristic. As a result, resilience is a teachable skill that occurs at any age and at any level, meaning that resilience is not an inherent phenomenon, but is achieved through practice, training, learning and experience. During a storm, some snow trees weigh on their branches and bend, but they do not break, and as soon as the storm subsides and the snow melts, these trees gradually rise and grow stronger than before.

Also, in the life of some people, despite growing up in a not so suitable environment, they have achieved great success in their lives, or conversely, people who have many facilities and ideal conditions, have achieved little success in life.

In fact, it can be said that in the daily life of human beings, the nature of some conditions and experiences is such that people inevitably get into trouble in such a way that their mental health may be threatened. Resilience includes a set of individual and psychological capacities with the help of which a person can resist in difficult situations and not be harmed, and even improve himself / herself as a result of these critical and difficult conditions.

How to become resilient?

You may ask, what exactly does a person do in resilience? Instead of focusing on the problem, the resilient person focuses more on their problem-solving abilities and even tries to use the situation as an opportunity.

So, resilience allows one to solve problems very well, not to run away from them. In short, resilience is used for those who are at risk, but do not have mental disorders and their lives are not disturbed, and if possible, quickly return to the previous balanced situation. Resilience allows people in difficult situations and despite the risk factors to use their existing capacities to achieve success and growth of individual life and use these challenges and tests as an opportunity to empower themselves and use them. Come out proud.

Factors enhancing resilience

Resilience enables people to face the hardships and difficulties of life without being harmed and even to use these opportunities to develop their personality. Factors that increase resilience include the following:

- ✓ Having high self-esteem plays an important role in coping with life stresses. If you believe in your abilities, you will be much more effective in dealing with life's problems.
- ✓ Have meaning and purpose in your life.
- ✓ Develop your relationships, so having strong emotional and social relationships is a very important factor in a person's mental health and healthy lifestyle.
- ✓ Be flexible about change.
- ✓ Take care of your nutrition and health.
- ✓ Learn healthy living skills to deal with problems.
- ✓ Be optimistic, that is, do not forget to look realistically with positive thinking, have good thoughts and hope for the future.
- ✓ Create positive attachments, that is, participating in one or more healthy recreational activities, membership in religious groups, attending sports clubs, art classes, science societies, and any activity that interests you can be very helpful. Be.
- ✓ Strengthen your spirituality, so people who have strong faith in problems and hardships rely on God while trying and reasoning.

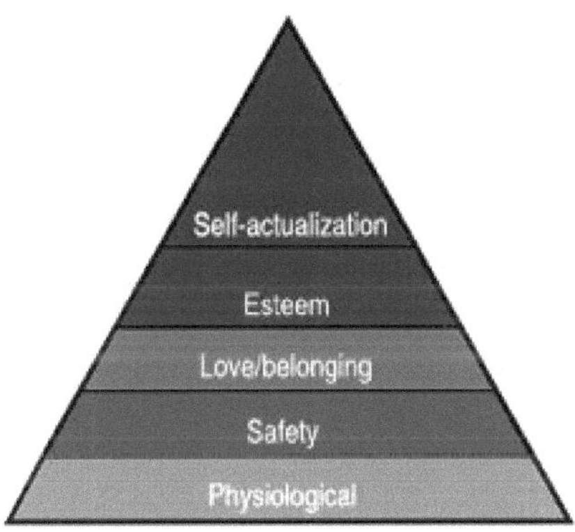

Figure 26. Maslow's Hierarchy of Needs

Healthy lifestyle in adulthood

Healthy lifestyles in adulthood help adults to move on with a more vibrant and relaxed life and to lead successful personal and social lives. Unhealthy diet, inadequate sleep, smoking, alcohol and drugs, inactivity and unprotected sex put people at risk. A healthy lifestyle in adulthood means that people eliminate the things mentioned in their lives or can control them to some extent. In other words, in order for people to stay healthy and be safe from a variety of diseases, they must have a healthy lifestyle.

Different solutions for a healthy lifestyle

A) **Have a healthy diet:** Learn about the composition of healthy foods and inform those who live with you. In fact, eat a healthy diet, such as reducing your salt intake, reducing your fat intake, and reducing your sugar intake. Eat in moderation and learn to distinguish true hunger from eating due to boredom or stress.

B) Keep your weight in the right position: If you need to lose weight, commit to a long-term change in eating habits, not just a temporary diet. Set a reasonable and balanced diet for yourself. Eat small amounts at each meal and exercise regularly. In other words, keep your body weight in the right position.

C) Observe sleep hygiene: Adequate rest and sleep is necessary to maintain and promote physical and mental health, maintain and promote mental strength and optimal growth and development. In fact, the body can regenerate and empower itself with enough rest and sleep. Sleep has at least two benefits, one is maintaining energy because people are resting and getting ready for a variety of activities throughout the day, and the other is revitalizing the brain, a process that clears daily trivia of the brain and prepares people for a new day.

D) Maintain your fitness: Choose a specific time for exercise and commit to it. Exercise with your spouse or friend and encourage each other to continue physical activity and make it more enjoyable. Have reasonable expectations and take enough time to achieve fitness and fitness. Many people give up sports because they have very ambitious expectations.

E) Do not smoke or drink: Try not to drink. Do not allow yourself to feel the need to drink to be accepted or to enjoy a social event. If you are a smoker, choose a stress-free time to quit. Also, get support from your spouse or someone you can count on for help.

F) Control stress: Balance work, family, and leisure. Be aware of stressors and identify ways to deal with them so that you can be more prepared when they occur. Exercise regularly and take time to rest and think every day.

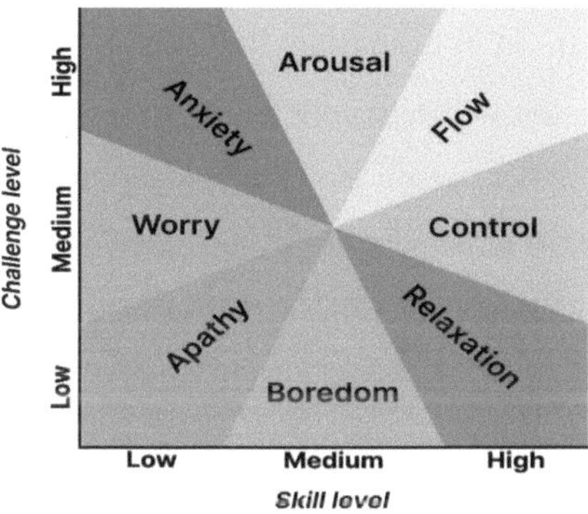

Figure 27. Apathy

G) Manage your sexual behavior: Sex is one of the main instincts for human survival, but it can be a way for pathogens to enter. Sexually transmitted infections are infections that are transmitted through sexual contact. There are more than 30 known pathogens that can be transmitted through sexual contact. Change your attitudes and behaviors to build a cordial relationship. Learn about anatomy and sexual function to protect yourself from sexually transmitted diseases such as gonorrhea and syphilis.

Psychology and communication skills

Man is a social being and needs to communicate with each other. Communicating effectively is a skill that must be learned. Communication is the process of sending and receiving verbal and non-verbal messages. Verbal communication has a smaller share of non-verbal communication in the communication process, but is very important in its place. Communication in general is the process by which we express our thoughts, ideas, feelings, and emotions, and receive the thoughts and feelings of others.

1- Communication skills

Communication is the process of sending and receiving messages. According to this definition, any communication requires the presence of two or more social units, i.e., communication can take place between two or more people, one person and one media, and so on. The main purpose of communication is to convey a message that can be conveyed verbally or non-verbally. In fact, a message can be conveyed explicitly or implicitly. Any problem in transmitting the message can cause communication problems. For example, the message may not be fully conveyed, or one person may send a message but the other person may receive another message, or someone may even send a message but the other person may not receive any message, usually referred to as " This is called a "misunderstanding". Communication skill is communication that closes the way to possible misunderstandings. In general, communication skills are one of the main skills in life that help shy people to be able to communicate better with others.

2- Communication components

Communication has different aspects. Communication components include verbal and non-verbal content. Verbal elements of communication include that aspect of communication that is specifically related to verbal content and the process of verbal expression. The content of the word means what we say. Non-verbal elements of communication include that aspect of communication that relates to aspects other than verbal content and the process of verbal expression, which can include tone of voice, tone of voice, eye contact, facial expressions, gestures, body postures. And called listening. Verbal communication means talking to others. This dimension covers a very small part of communication. In effective verbal communication, people can speak freely and in appropriate sentences about their expectations and feelings, express their requests, and ask others to change their behavior.

A) Expressing expectations: The tool of desires and expectations is an important component in the relationship and intimate relationships of which marital relationships are a part. To express expectations, the following simple sentences can be used:

- ✓ I expect that ...
- ✓ My request is that ...

B) Expressing emotions: Expressing emotions is very important in interpersonal and marital relationships. This is not a difficult task and if you practice, you can easily express your positive and negative feelings like extroverts. In fact, it is the expression of love and affection that brings couples closer together. Expressions of resentment and resentment also bring couples closer together and prevent the emotional bond between them from weakening. It is better to use sentences that start with "I" to express emotions

- ✓ I feel angry
- ✓ I am sad

C) Asking: One of the signs of effective communication is that both parties can easily make their requests. The best way to request is to use words like please, please, and so on. Asking for behavior change is one of the most important parts of verbal communication and is very important in marital relationships. It is better to ask another to change his behavior in a three-part sentence. The first part can be the feeling of the person, the second part describes the behavior of the other party and the third part is the expression of expectation. Of course, the first and second parts can be moved. for example:

- ✓ I'm sorry you're late and you do not know I expect you to let me know in advance.
- ✓ When you speak, you interrupt me and it upsets me, I expect you to let me finish.

3- Barriers to verbal communication

A) Not listening: When someone is talking and you are not listening, it means that there is an obstacle in the way of effective communication. The other party feels that you do not care much about him.

B) Inappropriate literature: The use of inappropriate words and sentences causes misunderstandings. In many cases, people say that inappropriate literature on verbal communication has damaged their self-esteem.

C) Do's and don'ts: Do's and don'ts are binding. The do's and don'ts we use for others can lead to misunderstandings and tensions in interpersonal relationships. For example, you should help me or you should not be late. One way to reduce stress in a marital relationship is to avoid using the do's and don'ts. Instead, you can use the words "better" or "not better". Like "Isn't it better to let me know before it's too late?"

4- Hidden content (non-verbal)

Non-verbal communication is an important part of communication. Characteristic of nonverbal listening communication is the attention to facial expressions and limbs and body language, which are described below:

A) Listening: Listening is different from hearing. When you listen, you pay attention, you look, you have a presence of mind, and your facial expressions show the speaker that you are listening. Barriers to listening include daydreaming, not looking, working while listening, judging the speaker, being entertained by a cell phone, and so on.

B) Facial postures: Facial postures include items such as tone of voice, tone of voice, eyebrow movements, mockery, grin, and gaze.

C) Posture: Posture How to use your hands, how to walk and sit can disrupt the relationship. Suppose someone is talking and the listener plays with his hands or shakes his head around, walks, etc. Recognizing body language helps people communicate more effectively.

5- Barriers to non-verbal communication

- ✓ Looking around (disinterested)
- ✓ Raising eyebrows (opposing)
- ✓ Squeezing the lips and teeth
- ✓ to frown
- ✓ Knocking finger on the table (impatient)
- ✓ Keep yourself away from the person
- ✓ Lean back and move away from the speaker
- ✓ Not expressing any encouragement such as locking hands and arms, folding legs to compose oneself, trembling hands, trembling legs (as a sign of fear) and ...
- ✓ Cold and soulless greetings
- ✓ Stay still
- ✓ No physical contact in general

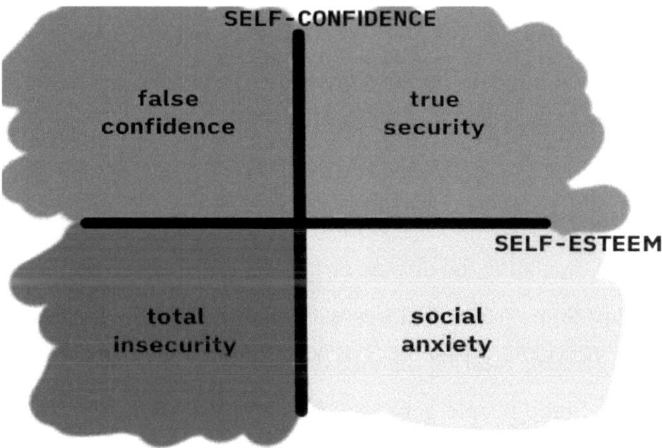

Figure 28. Self-Esteem, Self-Confidence and Anxiety

Psychology and Conflict Resolution

A dispute between two or more people is called a conflict. It is natural to be in conflict with others, because we are all different. Because human beings are naturally different and different in their views of others and issues, it is natural for them to be in conflict with each other. Disputes between couples are inevitable. Not having conflict does not necessarily mean having a better relationship. Because differences are not bad or good in themselves, but how they are resolved can lead to differences or lead to problem solving and intimacy. In general, this skill is one of the life skills and people should learn it.

1- Conflict resolution methods

Human beings are social beings, and while they need to be together, they inevitably have differences in desires and goals in relation to each other. Differences in any relationship are inevitable.

Conflict resolution methods fall into two categories:

A) Unhealthy methods of conflict resolution;

B) Healthy methods of conflict resolution.

A) Unhealthy methods of conflict resolution: Unhealthy methods of conflict resolution include avoiding conflict resolution, severing the relationship, coercing the relationship, coercing, leaving the problem over time, falling short and aggressive behavior:

- ✓ Avoiding conflict: In this case, people refuse to talk about conflict. The reason is the fear of escalating the dispute or lack of skills to resolve the conflict.
- ✓ Breaking up: Some people cut ties with another due to a dispute with another. Such a thing means clearing the face of the issue.
- ✓ Harassment: Some people get angry because of differences. Harassment is an avoidance method for resolving disputes and does not solve the problem.
- ✓ Passing the problem over time: Some people leave their differences with others over time so that they may resolve themselves over time. This method is also not effective, because there are many people who were angry with each other for years due to differences, but the differences are still there.
- ✓ Shortcuts: Another way to resolve conflict is to shorten. When we fall short of those with whom we disagree, it does not mean that the dispute has been resolved, but it means that we have violated our right for some reason.
- ✓ Aggressive Behavior: Some people become aggressive following a dispute with another, for example, they swear, start a fight, and so on.

B) Healthy Conflict Resolution Methods: The golden key to a healthy conflict resolution method is "negotiation". Negotiation is a conversation between two or more people with a specific goal, which is usually to reach a solution or resolve a dispute. Negotiation requires the speaker to speak carefully, clearly, and simply, and to allow the other person to do the same. Negotiations must take place in the right atmosphere and at the right time, and the two sides must be in good spirits. Tiredness, hunger and headaches cannot lead to a good negotiation.

- ✓ Listening: Listening is different from hearing. When you listen to someone, you are paying attention and listening. This behavior makes the speaker feel that you care about him or her and that you listen carefully. In the process of resolving a dispute, listening carefully will help you become familiar with the other party's point of view. This reduces the likelihood of misunderstanding in interpersonal relationships.

- ✓ Allowing someone else to talk: Negotiation, as its name implies, is a two-way conversation. Both sides should give each other a chance to talk.
- ✓ During another conversation, listen carefully and do not interrupt the other party.
- ✓ Dealing with the problem and not looking for the culprit: Effective negotiation requires two people to address the problem and its solutions, be critical but not looking for the culprit.
- ✓ Seeking guilt is one of the most important barriers to negotiating to resolve a dispute.
- ✓ Provide solutions: Problem and dispute resolution is possible by providing solutions from both parties. Therefore, the two sides in the negotiation must offer solutions and pay attention to another point of view in presenting solutions.
- ✓ Dealing with one problem (no more) It is not possible to solve all problems in one session. Therefore, it is better to choose the most important issue and discuss it. After resolving one problem, you can move on to another.
- ✓ Empathy: Empathy means putting yourself in the other person's shoes and looking at the issue from their point of view. Looking at it from another angle helps you to consider the interests and satisfaction of the other party in providing solutions.

Figure 29. Personality Development Courses in Navi Mumbai

- ✓ Separating feelings from behavior: You may not feel good about the person you are negotiating with. If you are going to involve your emotions, negotiation will not go well. The best thing to do is not to get caught up in the negotiation process and focus on the problem and look for solutions to the problem.
- ✓ Using a pause technique: This technique is used when two people lose their composure and kindness during a conversation and become angry. In fact, the two sides should be taught to temporarily end the conversation before they get angry so that they can calm down. Example: "I think we'd better end the conversation right now. We're both tired and nervous right now, and I don't think now is a good time to talk. Let's move on when we find peace again."
- ✓ Applying the win-win method: When giving a solution, think about the end goal. The ultimate goal is to solve the problem and improve the relationship. If the solutions offered only serve your interests and ignore the interests of the other party to the negotiation, the consent of the other party will never be provided and as a result the negotiation will be useless. The best option is to offer solutions that serve both your interests and the interests of others.

Conflicts and types of win-win methods

A) Lottery: When two people agree on the implementation of a solution, but they disagree on who will do something first, the lottery solves the problem.

B) Taking turns: When the two parties have trouble doing something together, it takes time, and thus each has to take action in turn. For example, if there is a dispute between two people over washing dishes, they can take turns solving the problem. In such a way that the days of one couple and the days of another person wash the dishes.

C) Third party arbitration: When both parties to the negotiation do not reach a solution or both insist on a solution that is in their favor, arbitrating a third party facilitates the negotiation process. A white beard, a trusted person or a friend can be asked to judge between two people and suggest options to resolve the dispute. Of course, the referee must also suggest options that are in the best interest of both parties, not one of the parties.

What are the factors that hinder effective negotiation?

Not listening, interrupting another, speaking in an inappropriate tone, speaking loudly, instead of addressing the other person's problem, condemning several problems at the same time, sticking to the other and judging him, himself Wanting and pursuing only one's own interest, dishonesty and secrecy, ignoring other words, acting in one's own favor and pursuing solutions that do not have much advantage for the other party, finding fault with the other, diverting the subject of discussion, Underestimating each other's feelings, humiliating each other, talking to inappropriate literature, facial expressions and inappropriate nonverbal behaviors, and presenting past problems are all major barriers to negotiation.

What factors facilitate negotiation?

Factors that facilitate negotiation include: acknowledging the other person's feelings, summarizing his or her speech, empathizing and paying attention to the other person's point of view and feeling, focusing on the problem rather than the person, focusing on the current problem rather than past problems, expressing feelings, expectations, needs Self and allowing the other to express his feelings, expectations and needs.

Psychology and empathy skills

When you empathize with another person, you may feel sorry for him or her, and this shows that there is still a gap between him or her, but when you are empathetic, in addition to knowing how he or she is feeling, you are feeling that way. You understand and feel it with him. As Weizgik puts it: The definition of empathy refers to feeling with another person, not feeling sorry for him.

For example, when it comes to the difference between empathy and empathy, if one of your friends experiences the grief of a loved one, the appropriate and empathetic response is to try to put ourselves in his or her shoes and find out how he or she feels, not feel sorry for him or her.

In today's society, empathy is a declining art. Life has become so hectic and confusing that it is difficult to feel what is going on around it. The less aware we are of the moment, the more difficult it becomes to be in tune with the feelings and goals of others. At the same time, empathy is essential for healthy relationships and the development of social skills.

Through empathy, we can accurately experience another person's inner conflicts, emotional pain, and inner world. When we do not have empathy, we cannot understand others and as a result we never know the people we interact with deeply. While having this skill helps us to resolve conflicts better and have more mature relationships with others. Fortunately, the development of empathy in childhood does not stop and we can cultivate it throughout life.

Certainly, strengthening this skill is not like walking in a park and requires a lot of practice and concentration, but it is not impossible. You can develop this ability by using the following strategies, but before that you need to know the difference between empathy and the importance of improving empathy skills.

What are the benefits of improving empathy skills?

At first, when you practice empathy, you naturally gain a deeper understanding of other people's behaviors, motivations, and life experiences, so you can better sense people's desires and needs. This in turn helps you to connect with people on a deeper level to have stronger bonds and more lasting relationships with others.

Regarding the benefits of improving empathy skills, it is important to know that the higher the level of the relationship, the more trust is formed between you and the other person. As a result, the level of coordination increases and helps you resolve disputes much faster. For this reason, increasing empathy and paying attention to the needs of the other party is one of the keys to success in any relationship, whether in marriage or work. Active listening is the most important step in strengthening empathy.

Strategies to strengthen empathy

Most of us have a laid-back attitude when it comes to painting a picture about ourselves. In fact, the most important skill among the ways to strengthen the skill of empathy with others is active listening. In this way, the first person listens and speaks only when he has heard and understood other words carefully. Active listening can give others the feeling that they are being heard and understood by you, and in addition to helping you have a successful marriage, it is also very effective in advancing your working relationship. This skill has five steps:

1- Active listening

Listen more than you talk. Most of us have a laid-back attitude when it comes to painting a picture about ourselves. He listens carefully to what others have to say. This skill is called active listening. For example, when talking to your spouse, you can use these five steps:

- ✓ Stay committed to the conversation. This means that you should not use a mobile phone, tablet or computer and show that you are fully aware of the conversation by maintaining eye contact with someone else.
- ✓ Let the speaker really speak. Give the other person time to finish his thoughts and refrain from jumping on his words.
- ✓ Summarize what you understand. When the speaker has finished speaking, summarize your understanding of what he or she is saying, and then ask, "Did I get it right?"
- ✓ Ask clarifying and relevant questions. Use your natural curiosity and ask questions that are not to be judged. This way you can better understand the other person's views, thoughts and feelings.
- ✓ Let the other say whatever he wants. Someone who is in trouble may be emotionally disturbed, and there is nothing wrong with that. Give her space to feel it.
- ✓ Let her speak from the bottom of her heart and share her feelings with you. This allows the individual to discover the solutions themselves.

The best function of active listening is that although people find a solution after talking to their empath, they often attribute the process to the person who empathizes with them. So even if you talk too little in the conversation, your spouse will not see it that way. Many times, the purpose of talking is not to reach a solution, but to share feelings and thoughts. This reduces the psychological burden of the problem they are facing and allows them to look at the problem more openly, and can eventually even lead to finding a solution. That is why the skill of active listening is one of the most important skills in increasing empathy in any type of relationship, whether marriage or work.

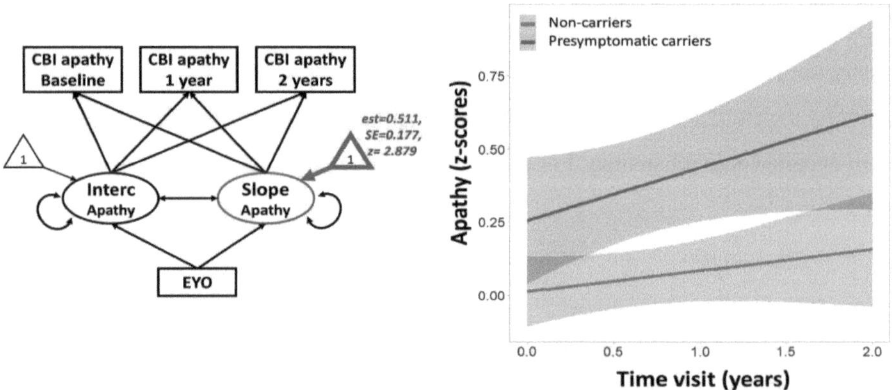

Figure 30. Apathy in pre-symptomatic genetic frontotemporal dementia predicts cognitive decline

After listening to other words, there is a great opportunity to express empathy and also to say how you would feel if you were in that situation. Expressing these views is a good way to express your feelings and a way to strengthen your empathy skills with others. The important thing is that these statements are real, not artificial. So, try to imagine exactly what the other person is in.

Put your foot in another shoe and imagine for a moment that this has happened to you and let the emotions guide you. This method is also very effective for good communication with the child. Express feelings as soon as you put yourself in the other person's shoes. In many cases, your emotional response will be similar to theirs, and this will make the other person feel that they are understood and heard, and a stronger connection is formed between you. Vulnerability makes people feel like they are and has a huge impact on strengthening relationships.

People feel that others have weaknesses and fears just like themselves, and as a result they realize that they are not alone in experiencing these feelings. In other words, do not be afraid to ask for help. Asking for help shows vulnerability, and vulnerability often leads to a stronger sense of connection. For example, suppose your friend has a problem or a failed love affair in an emotional relationship.

At first, as you listen carefully to your friend, try to think of a time when you were in a similar situation. For example, you may have had problems in your emotional relationship in the past. Remember how you felt in that situation. You may experience feelings of worry and anxiety at the time and not be able to cope well. Share these feelings with the other person, then share what you learned in that situation with the other person. Hypotheses are the enemy of empathy.

Hypothesis building means resorting to predetermined concepts that are not based on real understanding or experience. Most of us have a laid-back attitude when it comes to painting a picture about ourselves, but when we do, we can't see the whole picture. As a result, we do not really solve the problem, if this skill is part of life skills. When you hypothesize, your perception can rarely be well matched to the problem the person is facing. As a result, the relationship you want to have with someone else seems forced and unnatural.

It is not surprising that when you make a hypothesis, the other person thinks to himself that he does not understand my situation or that he is not someone I will ask for help in the future, because he does not listen at all. So do not rush into empathy and do not try to empathize before you truly understand the situation. Take five minutes to listen carefully and ask questions before trying to communicate with the other person.

The relationship between imagination and empathy

The problem is that you do not have to experience all the situations to be able to empathize, but you do need to be able to put yourself in the other person's shoes. The ability to imagine what another person is feeling is essential, even if we have not experienced it ourselves. To learn empathy, we need to strengthen our imagination. If you enjoy reading, pick up a book and focus on the characters' feelings and behaviors while reading. Some of the writings of classical literature, such as Hamlet Shakespeare, can be useful studies for understanding the full range of human emotions. Use your imagination to put yourself in the characters' shoes and understand their feelings and thoughts.

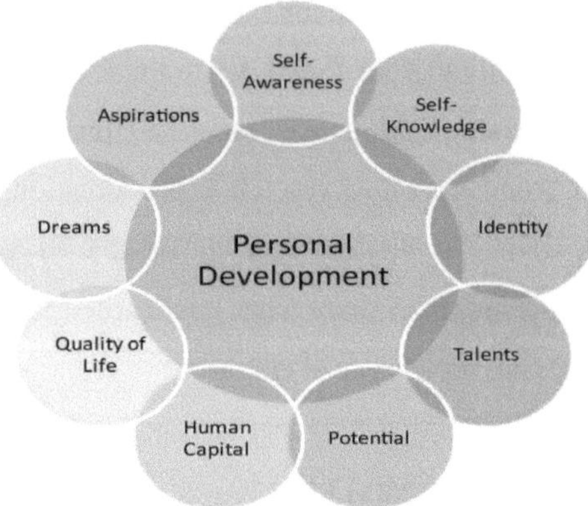

Figure 31. Developing Self Awareness

Psychology and self-awareness skills

1- Defining self-awareness skills

One of the most important factors that help a person to have a good and successful life is to know himself, to feel good about himself and to be happy and satisfied with what he is. Self-awareness is one of life skills.

This skill helps a person to know more about himself, his characteristics, needs, wants, goals, weaknesses, strengths, feelings, values and identity. Studies show that poor self-awareness is associated with many diseases and psychosocial injuries. Among the psychosocial problems associated with poor self-awareness, we can mention depression, anxiety, feelings of inferiority, low self-esteem, communication problems, feelings of loneliness, substance abuse, escape, and so on. Therefore, acquiring self-awareness skills is very important to prevent the above types of problems. Self-awareness is also one of the basic skills for fostering resilience.

In defining self-awareness skills, we can say that self-awareness means the ability to recognize and understand needs, weaknesses, desires, recognizing capabilities, recognizing attitudes, recognizing beliefs, recognizing talents, recognizing goals, recognizing values, recognizing desires, habits and any other aspect.

Which shapes a person's behavior? Self-awareness is one of the five components of emotional intelligence. Self-knowledge has a great impact on human success. People can also realistically set goals for their lives. People who are self-aware value themselves and others and do not humiliate and blame themselves and others. They are also interested in consulting with others and consulting with themselves and others. In general, it can be said that people reach a correct and logical image of themselves by reaching self-awareness and can have a happy and successful life. People who are highly self-aware and know themselves well usually have common characteristics, some of which are mentioned below:

- ✓ Recognize their positive qualities and abilities and talents and be proud of them.
- ✓ Recognize their negative characteristics and weaknesses, accept them and try to correct them.
- ✓ They know their successes and failures and are proud of their successes and learn from their failures.
- ✓ Respect themselves and others.
- ✓ They strive to achieve their goals.
- ✓ They take responsibility for their actions and behavior.

Figure 32. International Community - self awareness

2- The importance of self-awareness skills

Using self-awareness skills, you can identify, be aware of, and control your emotions. Inability to control emotions can lead to delinquency, addiction, violence, conflict with others, abuse and violence with others, especially children and adolescents. In addition, you can be aware of your strengths and weaknesses and reduce your weaknesses by relying on your strengths. Awareness of weaknesses allows a person to use this awareness to have more control over themselves.

On the other hand, self-awareness helps you become aware of your needs and find healthy ways to meet your needs. By knowing your needs, you can find a better way to meet your needs. Regarding the importance of self-awareness skills, it is necessary to know that by having this skill, you can become aware of your valuable criteria and find your value in life. In this way, avoid pursuing false values and live your life with more satisfaction and peace.

Carry out your identification process in a healthy way. Achieving a healthy identity builds an adult life on a solid foundation. You can also set realistic goals for your life, thus pursuing very idealistic, imaginative, and perfectionist goals. Choose away. Setting unrealistic goals leads to delinquency, failure, anger and violence, suicide, promiscuity and the like.

3- The main areas of self-awareness

Humans are complex and diverse. To become more self-aware, we need to increase our understanding in many areas. The main areas of self-awareness include personality traits, personal values, habits, feelings, and psychological needs that affect how we behave.

A) Personality: We usually change our personality, values and needs based on what we learn about ourselves, but understanding our personality helps us find situations in which we will thrive. It also prevents us from being in extremely stressful situations. For example, if you have the characteristics of an introvert and you want to work in a job that does not fit your personality, such as a salesperson, you need to learn regular skills with extroversion. Self-awareness helps you better analyze such decisions.

B) Values: It is very important for each of us to focus on our personal values. For example, if your priority is spending time with your child or worshiping, it is easier for you to decide what to prioritize in everyday situations. During working hours, there are many problems and opportunities that expand our to-do list and we may not be able to do them all due to working hours, but when our priorities are clear, we can do so. Make better decisions and do the things that matter most first.

C) Habits: Habits are behaviors that we do regularly and often automatically. Although we like to have habits that help us communicate and manage others, we can probably all identify at least one of our habits that reduces our effectiveness. For example, if you are a manager who never consults your employees before making decisions, this habit may negatively affect employees' commitment and decision-making skills.

D) Needs: Maslow and other scientists have identified and proposed a variety of psychological needs that motivate our behavior with the needs of self-esteem, love, sense of belonging, progress, power, self-awareness and control. One of the benefits of knowing what needs to have the most impact on our behavior is that it helps us understand how these needs affect our relationships with others. For example, many of us know people who are in dire need of high positions. These people are attracted to jobs that have a high social status and are looking for great positions in their organizations. Such people want things that show their status. They insist on being respected and sometimes fight for things that others find futile.

E) Emotions: Emotional self-awareness has recently become a hot topic because it is one of the five dimensions of emotional intelligence. Understanding your emotions, their factors, and their impact on your thoughts and behaviors reflects emotional self-awareness. A person with high emotional awareness understands the internal process associated with emotional experiences and therefore has more control over their emotions.

The Four Self-Awareness Archetypes

This 2x2 maps internal self-awareness (how well you know yourself) against external self-awareness (how well you understand how others see you).

	Low external self-awareness	High external self-awareness
High internal self-awareness	**INTROSPECTORS** They're clear on who they are but don't challenge their own views or search for blind spots by getting feedback from others. This can harm their relationships and limit their success.	**AWARE** They know who they are, what they want to accomplish, and seek out and value others' opinions. This is where leaders begin to fully realize the true benefits of self-awareness.
Low internal self-awareness	**SEEKERS** They don't yet know who they are, what they stand for, or how their teams see them. As a result, they might feel stuck or frustrated with their performance and relationships.	**PLEASERS** They can be so focused on appearing a certain way to others that they could be overlooking what matters to them. Over time, they tend to make choices that aren't in service of their own success and fulfillment.

Figure 33. Self-Awareness: Top Benefits, Dumb Mistakes & Key Takeaways

4- Ways to increase self-awareness skills

Self-awareness is a skill that anyone can learn with the right practice and habits. Are there parts of your life or personality that you do not seem to understand? Do you have certain behaviors or tendencies that often appear in you despite the negative consequences? The ability to be self-aware is one of the most vital and at the same time the most difficult skills that people can achieve. Many people feel that they have a healthy self-awareness, but it is better to look at it relative and see how much you have this ability compared to others. Self-awareness creates an opportunity to change one's behavior and beliefs. This change in mental state also changes your emotions and increases your emotional intelligence, which is an important factor in achieving success. Learning how to become more self-aware is an important step in creating the life you want.

Psychology and persuading others

There are different psychological theories in different groupings to convince. In the following, we will describe each of these methods. You are all familiar with these methods and use them in your relationships.

1- Intensification and reinforcement hypothesis

When you express a particular attitude with confidence, that attitude is reinforced. The opposite is also true. If you present an attitude with insecurity, that attitude will weaken in you.

2- Theory of transformation and change

Minorities in any group can have indirect effects on the majority. People in the majority group who are more sensitive and ready to be accepted are influenced by the minority group because they see this acceptance as simple or they have no other choice. When minorities are united, they will have a loud voice.

3- Theory of information manipulation

In this hypothesis, a person who has a great ability to persuade breaks the usual principles and rules in conversation, which are in the following four forms:

A) Quantity: Extensive and complete information is presented.

B) Quality: Accurate and accurate information is provided.

C) Communication: Information related to the topic of conversation is presented.

D) Mode: Information is expressed in a simple way and body and non-verbal movements are used for further explanation.

4- Chinese Introduction

Short-term thoughts and actions of people with a stimulus can be affected. So, a conscious and correct Chinese introduction can be effective in persuading others. Grounding for your profession has a great impact on its acceptance towards the audience.

5- The norm of transaction is like

Social norms force us to react appropriately to the behavior of the people who accompany us. Of course, bargaining is a positive form of retaliation, that is, we tend to reciprocate the kindness shown to us by others.

6- The principle of scarcity and rarity

Using some form of constraint to describe an issue or make a suggestion multiplies the desire for it. This principle manifests itself in the extraordinary auctions and sales that are offered in a limited period of time. You have probably experienced this principle in conversations as well. Feelings of limitation and fear of one's regret are examples of the principle of scarcity.

7- Sleeping effect

In this effect, a phenomenon occurs in which, despite the invalidity of the source of a message, the effects and acceptance of that message increase over time. In fact, over time, the message is institutionalized in the mind, and no one remembers that the source of such a message was not very credible.

8- Social effect

We are all influenced by the relationships we have with different people. For example, reference groups, people in the community who are superior to other members of the community in terms of privileges such as wealth, knowledge, and others, can influence others to be persuaded.

9- Yale attitude change approach

This theory came to fruition after years of research at Yale University. At Yale University, research was done on the factors that make up a good lecture. Factors that make the speaker more credible and engaging are whether the speaker makes the points at the beginning of the speech or at the end of the speech. Other persuasive factors and attention to the demographic structure of the audience and....

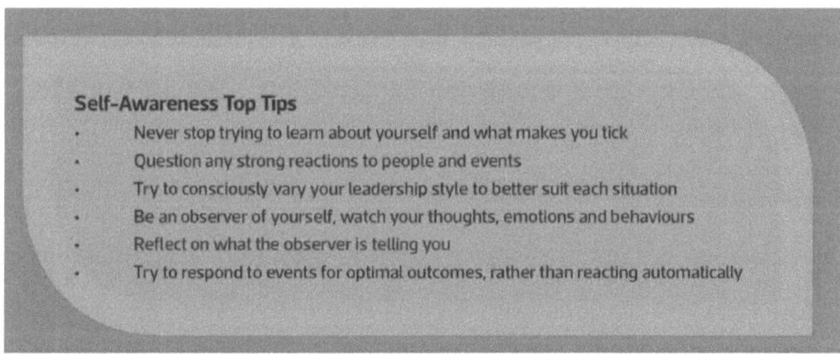

Figure 34. Authentic Leaders, The Institute of Leadership & Mgt

10- Final words and terms

Some words are more powerful than others. According to this theory, strong and persuasive words are divided into 3 categories:

A) Divine words: The semantic burden of these words is a state of prayer and request, and a kind of obedience and intercession is hidden in them. Growth and value are these words. Words that contain a kind of desire.

B) Evil words: words that express a kind of disgust and hatred. Like fascists, sadists and....

C) Attractive and charismatic words: These words carry a deeper and less intangible meaning than the previous two groups and are considered more meaningful. Such as freedom, participation and….

We all know the necessity and importance of basic needs such as food, heat, shelter and… for survival, but what are our needs after these basic necessities?

In the 1940s, Abraham Maslow proposed the pyramid of the hierarchy of human needs. In this pyramid, human needs are presented in 5 levels. Physical needs include food, water, rest, etc., security needs such as safety at work, health, family, etc., the need to love and belong like friends and relationships; Such as the possibility of expressing creativity and…. In this pyramid, the need for security, belonging and self-esteem has been raised, and marketing benefits the most from these three human needs, because without these three needs, our lives and functions will be disrupted. With the help of these 3 things, we can have emotional participation, express ourselves and our innovation. The better our needs are met in these three areas, the stronger and more successful we will be in our work, daily life, and relationships, and the better we will be able to persuade others in our relationships and even ourselves to advance different goals. The following miraculous phrases can also be used to create such a safe and acceptable atmosphere by the participants in each conversation: What if this is the case? This sentence makes various suggestions and seeks to add various solutions. It also eliminates selfishness and self-will in expressing opinions and explores different possibilities.

How is it possible to influence friends and audience?

To be an effective person in our relationships with our audience and friends, we must be able to build happy and positive relationships by reducing selfishness. Dale Carnegie, a psychology writer, suggests the following:

- ✓ The best way to handle conflict is to avoid it. So put aside the debate.
- ✓ Respect the opinions of others. Never tell others that you are wrong.
- ✓ If you make a mistake, accept it.
- ✓ Start your communication in a friendly way.
- ✓ Accompany others by saying affirmative words. For example, after the other person says something, say yes, yes.
- ✓ Allow others enough to talk.
- ✓ Allow others to participate in the process of generating ideas and opinions, so that everyone feels involved.
- ✓ Look at things from the point of view of others.
- ✓ Be sympathetic to the interests and opinions of others.
- ✓ Be open to new ideas and ideas.
- ✓ Make your comments appealing and audible.
- ✓ Face the challenges and smash them.

These points can also be used well in marketing and business. For example, in the field of marketing and advertising messages and writing titles, these communication points should be considered. Or it is better to use these tricks on websites. To be effective in your communication, you must remember that thanking, encouraging and praising others and apologizing works wonders. For example, if something went wrong in your business, you should apologize to the audience very quickly. Roger Dooley, for example, is a well-known blogger about neural marketing. He believes that the process of influencing people on others works like a sequel.

First, the person attracts another attention by climbing the sliding stairs and being in the sliding position, and begins the process of persuasion. Then attraction, which is the same as the initial and potential desire of the customer and the audience, causes the relationship to slip and begin.

The next step is to slide down the slope, which is actually the motivation you express to your audience and customer. These motivations are transmitted consciously or unconsciously.

Then, in the middle and final stage, there is a kind of friction and difficulty while sliding, and in fact, these are the communication challenges that must be properly managed. Stimulating the audience and the customer can be done through the various psychological methods mentioned in the previous lines. For example, reference groups are a good factor in attracting and persuading others to enter the persuasion and communication process.

Figure 35. Self-Awareness Needs Skills Values & Hopes

The principle of persuading others (Robert Caldini's view)

Robert Caldini is a writer who, in one of his books, Six Principles of Persuasion, outlines ways to better convince the audience. In his view, these steps and principles are as follows:

A) Bargain: The social norm Bargain.

B) Continuity: Reinforcement hypothesis.

C) Reference groups: social effect.

D) Interest: Social effect.

E) Authority and Power: An Approach to Changing Yale Attitudes.

F) Rarity and rarity: The principle of rarity and scarcity.

We inherently think that the things we love are powerful, and because we think they are rare, we are convinced sooner.

1- Interest

One of the most common ways in which people try to persuade and persuade others is through interest. For example, people ask each other, "Are you a football fan too?" "Yes, that's great." In this conversation, the persuasion process is smoother by touching on common points of interest. The same is true of business and advertising. For example, when you say that you are looking for more visitors to your website, you are actually looking to give in to the desire and interest of the customer. Such an alignment between the customer interest and your offer should be pursued in the next steps with real and practical action.

2- Power and authority

Expressing your credibility and power before entering the conversation and communication will make you more successful and acceptable in the next steps of convincing the audience. The more credible your credibility to the audience, the more impactful you will be.

3- Reference groups

Human beings have a greater desire than the work that is common and promoted in society by reputable people and guards. Reference groups can have a great impact on convincing other social groups. The principle of continuity and rarity is also very effective in the persuasion process.

For example, in the principle of continuity, with the help of reinforcement theory, you ask people about priorities in wants and needs, and according to the same needs and wants, you express your opinion and suggestion. In such a case, due to the active presence of the person in the formation, your opinion and suggestion, you will face less opposition and the percentage of acceptance of your profession will increase. In principle, like the extraordinary sales announced by stores, the customer quickly accepts the terms and conditions of the offer because of the time constraint of missing out on a great opportunity at certain intervals. These principles are very useful in normal life and business.

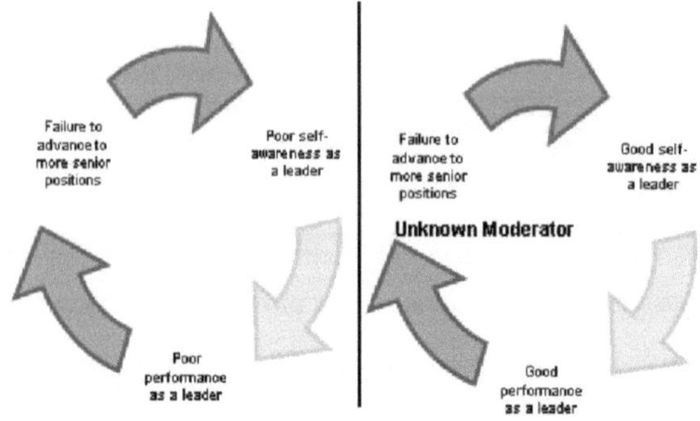

Figure 36. Theoretical model of female leaders' self-awareness

References

1. Assadollah, Farzatullah. (1997). Personality Psychology, Tabriz, Hadi Publishing, first edition.
2. Asadi Noghabi, Ahmad Ali (2005). Psychiatric Nursing (Behdasht Ravan 2), Tehran, Bashari.
3. Izadi, Sirus (2012). Personality psychology from the perspective of schools, Dehkhoda.
4. Bratos, Spencer; General Psychology, Tehran, 2005, seventh edition, pp. 27, 28.
5. Jeffrey, Young, and Closco, J. And Wishar, m. (2007). Schema therapy is a practical guide for clinical specialists (translated by Hamidpour, H. and Anduz, Z). Tehran: Arjmand Publications. Third edition. (No release date in the original language).
6. Zadok, Benjamin, Zadok, Virginia. (2006). Summary of Behavioral Psychology - Clinical Psychiatry, (translated by Hassan Rafiei and Farzin Rezaei). Tehran: Arjmand Publications. (No publication date in the original language).
7. Political, Ali Akbar (2010). Personality Psychology, Ibn Sina Publications.
8. Shamloo, Saeed (2011). "Schools and theories in personality psychology."
9. Schultz, Duane (2005). "Personality Theories", Yousef Karimi et al., Tehran, Arasbaran.
10. Rital L. Atkinson; Richard. s. Atkinson; Ernst R. Hilgard, 1983, translated by Mohammad Naghi Braheni et al., 1987, seventh edition, Roshd Publications, Tehran, page 35.
11. Schultz, Duane; History of Modern Psychology, Ali Akbar Seif, Tehran, University Press, 2012, Second Edition, pp. 294 and 293.
12. Sahebi, A. (2005). Cognitive therapy of personality disorders (schema-based approach), Tehran: Arjmand Publications.
13. Salavati, M. (2007). Dominant schemas and effectiveness of schema therapy in female patients with borderline personality disorder, PhD thesis in Clinical Psychology, Tehran Institute of Psychiatry, Iran School of Medical Sciences.
14. Azimi, Sirus; Principles of General Psychology, Tehran, Saffar, 2014, 16th edition, pp. 24, 25, 26.

15. Kaplan, Herlod, Zadok, Benjamin. (2010). Summary of Psychiatric Behavioral Sciences - Clinical Psychiatry, Volume I, (translated by Nusrat A. .... Pour Afkar). Tabriz Shahrab Water Publishing.
16. Karimi, Yousef (2001). "Personality Psychology", Institute of Opinion, p. 5 ...
17. Keith, M. David Sun. (2004). Application of cognitive therapy in personality disorders (translated by Shams, Giti). Tehran: Roshd Publications
18. Keith, M. David Sun. (2004). Application of cognitive therapy in personality disorders (translated by Shams, Giti). Tehran: Roshd Publications
19. Lotfi, Razia. (2006). Comparison of maladaptive schemas of healthy individuals and individuals with category B personality disorders, Master Thesis, University of Isfahan.
20. Leahy, Robert. (2008). Cognitive therapy techniques - guidance for psychotherapists, (translated by Laden Fati, Shima Shakiba and Hossein Naseri). Tehran: Danjeh Publishing. (No release date in the original language).
21. Madi, Salvatore, "Comparative analysis from the point of view of personality", translated by Ali Haghighi, ...
22. Mohammadzadeh, Ali. (2010). Investigating the relationship between schizotypal personality traits and ...
23. Maddie, Salvatore. (2015). A comparative analysis of personality theories, methods
24. Miziak, Henrik; History and schools of psychology, Ahmad Rezvani, Mashhad, Astan Quds Razavi, 1997, second edition, pp. 16 and 17.

Printed by Books on Demand GmbH, Norderstedt / Germany